Ever-Expanding Horizons

The

University

of

Massachusetts

Press

Amherst

1983

EVER-

The Dual Informational

EXPANDING

Sources of Human Evolution

HORIZONS

Carl P. Swanson

The publisher acknowledges permission to reprint selections from
material under copyright.
"Evolution" by May Swenson. From *New and Selected Things Taking Place*.
Copyright © 1954 by May Swenson. First appeared in *Discovery 3*.
By permission of Little, Brown and Company in association with
the Atlantic Monthly Press.
From George Gamow, *Matter, Earth, and Sky*, © 1965, p. 105.
Reprinted by permission of Prentice-Hall, Inc. Englewood Cliffs, N.J.
From Nan Fairbrother, *Man and Gardens*. Reprinted by permission of
the author's Literary Estate and The Hogarth Press, Ltd.
Designed by Mary Mendell

Contents

To my mother
Anna P. (Nordstrand) Swanson
in this, her 93d year
a small tribute to a great lady

Evolution

May Swenson, 1963

the stone
would like to be
Alive like me

the rooted tree
longs to be Free

the mute beast
envies my fate
Articulate

on this ball
half dark
half light
i walk Upright
i lie Prone
within the night

beautiful each Shape
to see
wonderful each Thing
to name
here a stone
there a tree
here a river
there a Flame

marvelous to Stroke
the patient beasts
within their yoke

how i Yearn
for the lion
in his den
though he spurn
the touch of men

the longing
that i know
is in the Stone also
it must be

the same that rises
in the Tree
the longing
in the Lion's call
speaks for all

oh to Endure
like the stone
sufficient
to itself alone

or Reincarnate
like the tree
be born each spring
to greenery

or like the lion
without law
to roam the Wild
on velvet paw

but if walking
i meet
a Creature like me
on the street
two-legged
with human face
to recognize
is to Embrace

wonders pale
beauties dim
during my delight
with Him

an Evolution strange
two Tongues touch
exchange
a Feast unknown
to stone
or tree or beast

Preface

THE GENESIS OF this volume can be traced back some eighteen years to my reading of an article by V. R. Potter (1964) in *Science,* in which he discussed briefly the notion that ideas are the cultural analogue of DNA, that is, that ideas are the source of cultural information as well as the basic units of cultural evolution. I had, by that time, begun to put together lecture material which eventually was published as *The Natural History of Man* (Swanson 1973). Potter's point of view continued to intrigue me, and although I had dealt with the problem only briefly and rather casually, I coined the term *sociogene* to identify those ideas that, maturing into shared concepts and interacting with the expressed information encoded in DNA, led to the emergence of the human phenotype with which we are all familiar. I still find the term appropriate.

Recently a number of well-known biologists as well as anthropologists have dealt with the nature, origin, and transmission of the elements that constitute culture in all its varied aspects. One can find both consensus and disagreement in these writings, a circumstance not wholly unexpected because the general subject matter is embraced by the hybrid and controversial term *sociobiology.* But this is all to the good, for as Nan Fairbrother (1956) once said in another connection:

every theory is useful if only to be disproved, for we can use it as a tool to turn over the unorganized mass of facts and arrange them in some kind of order. With a new subject we need lots of theories, one after the other, and as we pursue them and discard them we gradually get to know our material, like harrowing new ground first one way and then the other to break it up fine. It is only important to remember that our theories are only tools and not truths. In the end, when the ground is worked enough we must leave them behind in the tool-shed to go by ourselves with an open mind, and look again as if for the first time.

I find it of interest that none of these authors, in dealing with the evolution of man, has cited the work of Potter. Possibly they have not been stimulated by his article in the same way that I have; possibly what seemed new and novel to me was not to them. Be that as it may, recent interest in the cultural as well as the physical evolution of man suggests that cultural matters may possibly be illuminated by looking at them in the light of the more certain knowledge we have of the nature, function, and behavior of DNA. I have, therefore, confined my attention to a single, but not necessarily simple, question: What is the "DNA" of cultural evolution? In a sense the question asks for an expansion of the concept raised by Potter.

The whole subject of cultural origins and relationships touches us all in varied fashion. To those who are historically minded, it is a way of probing a past that is relatively uncluttered with tangible artifacts; to others it is like nuclear power, a potential source of information for use or abuse in human social affairs (Caplan 1978). Looked at broadly, it is an area where the disciplines of human paleontology, molecular genetics, cognitive psychology, and information theory seem to be finding common ground with the more familiar biological subdivisions of sensory physiology, comparative morphology, and animal behavior. Despite its controversial nature, sociobiology is indicative of this kind of integrative thinking. With a subject whose disciplinary limits are not yet well defined, new approaches, rearrangements of old and new data, and conjectural explorations are needed to provide different and possibly more illuminating frames of reference, to generate new questions, or to pose old questions in more precise terms. This brief volume, then, focuses its attention on a small but central part of human evolution, and attempts a cross-level comparison of the informational bases of organic and cultural evolution in an effort to discern commonalities as well as dissimilarities, possible homologies as well as analogies, and thereby to examine and to set in sharper focus the ways and means by which some of our human qualities were acquired and refined. My central thesis is that organic evolution in the vertebrate line leading to man has been characterized in the main by continually expanding perspectives and a more detailed dissection and assessment of the environment, accompanied by a continual improvement of the sensory and neural structures making such discernment possible. This is accomplished by evolutionary change taking place at a number of hierarchical levels: genome, cells, organs, organ systems, species, and populations. Cultural evolution operates similarly, although the units and levels differ. Ideas, concepts, philosophies, views of nature, and so forth are each expressed at individual, social, and multisocial levels. Information thus acquired through learning joins with that acquired through inheritance, and the genome and the nervous system come to be the two great parallel and interacting sources of evolving information which culminate in the appearance of man. If, in the process of analysis, I have shed any light on the problem, or have provoked any meaningful and fruitful discussion, well and good; if not, what I say here will quickly pass.

I have benefited by having the general topic of human evolution discussed by students in my own classes, as well as from comments made by some of my colleagues at the University of Massachusetts/Amherst who have read and criticized a brief essay I once wrote in an attempt to clarify my views to myself. I gratefully acknowledge this indebtedness, particularly to Professors David Mulcahy in Botany, Vincent Dethier in Zoology, Gordon Sutton in Sociology, and Harry Schumer and Charles Clifton in Psychology, some of who have encouraged me to turn the essay into book form. Such encouragement is essential for one like myself who does not comfortably and lightly enter a field of endeavor where one's knowledge may well be shallow and one's judgment suspect.

The bibliography at the end of this volume is a reflection of my reading and my biases, and an acknowledgment of my further debt to others who have published earlier: for information, ideas, points of view, even disagreements, the latter necessary for the better honing of my own thoughts. Whatever errors of fact, interpretation, and speculation might remain— and I have no illusions on this score—they are my responsibility.

C. P. Swanson

ONE

Introduction

HANGING IN THE Boston Museum of Fine Arts is a Tahitian scene by Paul Gauguin, one of the French artists of the postimpressionistic movement. Except for its rather large size, it is not conspicuously different from other Gauguin paintings of this same period and locale in the expressive and stark use of color, the deliberate flatness of perspective, and the unconcern, even inconsequentiality, of the individuals inhabiting the canvas. It is no particular scene in Tahiti at the turn of the century at the same time that it is the essence of all scenes, a symbol of an idea, of Gauguin's groping for elusive intangibles: the meaning of human existence, the questionable significance of its trappings, the uncertainty of its future, and the passive acceptance of its futility when hope fades, as it apparently did for him. These thoughts are embodied in the title that he gave to this painting—*Whence Do We Come? What Are We? Whither Are We Going?*—a title that would seem to bear but little relation to its content but that would be even more inexplicable without Gauguin's own appended explanation: "My eyes close in order to see *without understanding* the dream, in the infinite space that flies before me, and I perceive the mournful procession of my hopes" (his italics).

From chaos to order

The Gauguin vignette serves several purposes as we attempt to delineate the basis and mechanisms of cultural evolution, and to compare these with similar circumstances in organic evolution. In the first instance, it is representative of an attempt, and a rather involved one at that, by one human being to put some kind of order into the world as he sees it and, apparently, as he wishes others to see it as well. It is Gauguin's way of putting his knowledge, his experiences, and his emotions into a manageable, explicable, and functional whole. He has done so by selecting—from an infinite multitude of shapes, colors, and relations—those elements that have impressed themselves on his physical, biological, and psychological existence, and by expressing the emotions that are engendered by the interaction of the inner world of his being with the external world around him. It is an act that every sentient individual, of whatever species, engages in, intuitively or consciously, with the resultant manner and degree of expression depending upon the degree of sensitivity, flexibility, and responsiveness of that individual. It is what primitive man was doing at the time of his emergence from a protohuman state, and it is what we do today, as each of us tries to come to terms with his environment.

To organisms, living either singly or collectively as societies, chaos is biologically and psychologically intolerable, and an unordered environment is a form of chaos. Since every generation of organisms inevitably leaves its mark, great or small, on the environment, every succeeding generation must develop its own experiential and existential order from both the organized and unorganized potential of its time. It must do so in the face of what André Malraux called "the magnificent indifference of nature." If that order is to be functional, at all times it must be intimately related to the maintenance of a sense of equilibrium in a changing world over which the individual or the species can exercise but limited control. The pessimism of Gauguin indicates how difficult it is to express and maintain that state since it is based on abstract and often fleeting concepts of real or only imagined existence. The fact, however, is that no individual wanders naked and defenseless down the streets of experience. Nature has equipped each individual, and characterized each species, through programmed inheritance and/or piecemeal learning, with varying degrees of sensitivity for action and reaction to environmental variables, and with the cognitive and responsive abilities to aid in coping with the necessary, constant, and sometimes unexpected and unfamiliar demands of existence. Failure to cope means extinction, for the individual and for the species.

The Gauguin painting and statement further illustrate that oftentimes reality, as we come to know it, is not directly perceived but rather is what we imagine it to be. This is so because we are limited in our perception of the universe, the amount and kind of information we can handle, the concepts we are capable of formulating, and thus the problems we can solve (Sinsheimer 1971). We sense and hence imagine only that which we can encompass intellectually and psychologically, which means that vast segments of reality lie beyond our ken and are never a part of our existence. Indeed, the reality we perceive is an imagined reality, and its correspondence to the world around us may be close or quite remote. We have no absolute guidelines to help us here. Morowitz (1978) emphasized this when he stated that "our view of the physical universe is not a cold, lifeless abstraction but is structured by the human mind and the nature of life itself. While it has long been fashionable to inquire how biology depends on the underlying physics, we are being forced to inquire how physics depends on the underlying biology of the mind." Our world, therefore, is a series of isolated images, sequentially and selectively received. It is these images that, interacting with and modifying patterns of innate behavior, will form the basis of subsequent action, thought, and emotion. It is they that are the basis of culture, upon which cultural evolution acts and from among which further cultural selection takes place. All else is culturally derived: constructed tools, patterns of kinship, dietary habits, morals, the outward trappings that give visible form to a culture, and that to an observer distinguish one culture from another.

To perceive an image, as Gauguin perceived his, is to participate in a process of organization. In addition, to develop an
image consciously and to give it sufficient structure so that it
can be acted upon and transmitted—visually, verbally, or by
gesture—is to engage in a creative act. It implies the mental
ability to select, to measure, to interpret, to orient, even to abstract as we—as individuals, a society, or a culture—build our
organized world from the limited facets of our inheritance and
our experience. It is our sensory and nervous system confront-
ing the options available to it, and making choices. Some of our
images are limited by our biological inheritance (for instance,
the world of color is reduced to nuances of gray if we happen to
be color-blind). Some are acquired and fixed by rote learning at
impressionable, plastic, but authority-accepting stages of our
lives, or by the forces of tradition and custom (Sibatani 1980).
Still others we create throughout our lives and from our experiences, and since each of us is biologically unique, to that extent
do we create for ourselves a place in the ranks of culturally
unique individuals.

An unshared image is without effect; it dies with the individual like a mutation in one who is sterile. But we cannot share
images directly. We generally lack that sixth sense that some
claim to have, so we can only communicate images through a
medium of symbols that we invent as representatives of our
images. It would seem that the painted symbol of Gauguin was,
in his opinion, insufficient to convey to others the fragment of
the world he sought to depict in a cage of form, hence the title
he gave to his piece of art, followed by an additional explana-
tory note. A similar inadequacy of symbols to capture the essence of something apprehended was expressed recently by the
violinist Isaac Stern. Unwilling to have his rendition of a piece
of music, however beautiful and moving, stand alone, he
added, as he did in a radio conversation, that each of his performances was an attempt to portray, with utmost fidelity, the
"totality of an idea" that lay behind the music. The idea, the
image, was first in the mind of the composer, to be passed on to

others through the use of written symbols, then reinterpreted by the performer, and finally conveyed to the audience through the symbols of sound.

The use of symbols

As members of the animal kingdom, human beings stand out as image-formers and as symbolers. We are not alone in possessing this capability, but we are so adept that we are at an almost infinite remove from our nearest animal relatives. Symbols may be piled on symbols as we seek to put labels on reality and, by that process, to share mental images with each other in order to bridge the gap that separates the private world of individuals. Thus, like all of us, both Gauguin and Stern sought to express themselves through the means at their command, in their instance, through color and sound and words, and by the technical mastery with which they wielded their symbols so that we may share the shape and content of a fragment of their world. They describe worlds which some of us may sense intuitively or by training, but whose structures are made more tangible and self-evident by symbolic representation. These are ordered realities, fragments of a larger reality, whose contents and limits we seek to understand, if only because the alternative is meaningless chaos. The images we form and the symbols we use to express our imaginative gropings are a reflection of our inheritance, biological and cultural: of our experiences, our tastes, our imaginative abilities, and the constraints of the society within which each of us functions.

Images and symbols are, respectively, the fundamental bases and the tangible expressions of human culture. They are clearly related to each other, for a symbol that does not represent a comprehensible image is gibberish. There are, without question, feedback mechanisms that operate in the sense that symbols—the spoken word or rendered drawing, for example—can give form to but dimly apprehended images, but it is equally certain that mental imagery is the basis for our vision of the world around us.

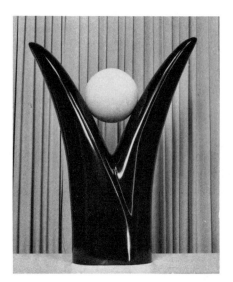

from earth
the mind
creates
the word

life given
life holding
life giving
a seed

thought grows
in the word
to plant
to field

to harvest
to new sowings

FIGURE I   *The Word, sculpture and poem by Thomas McGlynn (1970); the sculpture, of white marble and black Belgian marble, is four feet high (McAlister 1981).*

Both images and symbols are the tools of our cultural exist-ence, but we need to recognize that they are traps as well. As tools they are the means by which we order our experience, matching our observations, thoughts, and emotions with ap-propriate symbolic units so that they may be shared with oth-ers. But images are as selective as symbols are; we sense, think, feel, and express that which we have been taught to sense and think and feel and express, although it may be only a limited repertoire of what we are biologically capable. But both images and symbols are traps, for in selecting them we leave out that which is not selected. Our being and our existence are thereby circumscribed, culturally because we cannot participate in, let alone comprehend, all experiences, and biologically because we cannot escape beyond the limits of our inherited potential. However, our genetic and cultural attributes complement each other to give us a reality different from and expanded far be-yond that attainable by any other species, although that pla-

6

teau was reached through a continuum of change covering many millennia, and not by the sudden emergence of a unique and unshared quality. For example, we readily recognize that our biologically inherited receptor apparatus permits us to sense only a very limited portion of the electromagnetic spectrum, whereas our culturally advanced technology, developed and directed by our imaginative powers, can detect and analyze wave motion well beyond both ends of naturally perceived portions of the spectrum. In having the ability to thus expand our horizons we are unique among all animals. On the other hand, our bodies are kept in a physiological state of dynamic equilibrium by inherited detector and activator (homeostatic) mechanisms whose presence penetrates our consciousness only when we are under stress or when they fail to function properly. This property we share to varying degrees with all animal species.

Human evolution, therefore, results from the confluence of two systems of potential and exploitable information: our inherited genotypes which fit us structurally, physiologically, and behaviorally into the human species, and our nervous system, a product of our genetic endowment, which contributes behaviorally, but which can also transcend its origins and "learn behaviors congenial to itself" (Dethier 1982). Both of these systems contribute to the expression of human behavior, and it is behavior, broadly interpreted, that is selected for in the course of both biological and cultural evolution. As living organisms we cannot exist without genes, but as human beings we cannot do without images and symbols; our world, in short, is an imaginatively constructed reality, symbolically represented. As Geertz (1966) has so aptly expressed it: "Man needs such symbolic sources of illumination to find his way in the world because the unsymbolic ones that are constitutionally ingrained in his body cast so diffuse a light." We can look upon symbols—in contrast to material artifacts—as the first tangible evidence of the way by which, in communal fashion, our primitive ancestors handled the world around them as an imagined reality, and as that out of which our cultural heritage took its form. These symbols are also the more tangible ingredients of an evolution that, intermeshed with our organic inheritance, has provided the means that has led us out of our animality and into our humanity. To understand this duality we shall travel paths that are sometimes parallel and sometimes intersecting, in an effort to search out the origins of our godlike veneer within which the not-so-distant echoes of our animal past still reverberate.

Our dual inheritance

The very abstract basis of culture, however, suggests that exciting answers and new lines of inquiry are not likely to emerge from the examination of fossil remains or other artifacts. The search must be directed elsewhere, and new approaches and new hypotheses must be devised. This will include the renewing of acquaintance with long-standing and previously verified pieces of information in order to see them in a new context, the looking to neighboring disciplines for intriguing data and

FIGURE 2   *The dual pathways by which an individual or, collectively, a culture expresses itself through behavior.*

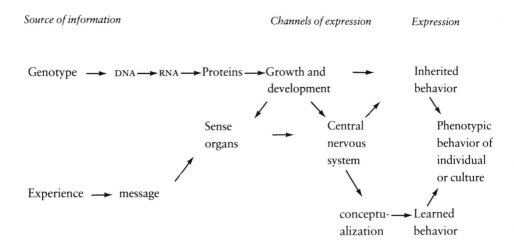

novel methods, and—when the period of history permits—the asking of different sets of questions. There is always the hope of coming up with different and possibly more illuminating answers to the problems of human origins.

The beginnings of this kind of shift in emphasis and perspective are evident today. Not only are traditional human paleontology and cultural patterns being vigorously explored and pursued, but new patterns of synthesis, new dimensions, and a new vitality seem also to be emerging. The substantive bases and theoretical extensions included within the area of human evolution are by no means clear or even broadly accepted by all concerned, but if the flood of writings that continue to be published is a genuine indication of intellectual ferment, we are witnessing the asking of different questions and the appearance of new ideas, bolstered by data from many peripheral fields. The recent volumes by Bonner (1980), P. J. Wilson (1980), Cavalli-Sforza and Feldman (1981), and Lumsden and Wilson (1981) seem particularly noteworthy for their offerings of stimulating approaches. Four of these authors are biologists, not anthropologists, and it seems most significant and promising that they bring their biological thinking and evolutionary philosophy into a discipline that traditionally has been less scientifically rigorous in method, content, and direction. The circumstances are reminiscent of the profound and widespread effect that physical thinking and methods had on the science of genetics in the 1950s and 1960s. This revolution has reshaped the whole structure of biology and, because of its novel thinking and practical applications, bids fair to extend its influence and philosophy far into the social and industrial areas of man. The discovery and understanding of the structure of deoxyribose nucleic acid (DNA) as the physical and informational basis of biological inheritance and organic evolution has provided us with an entirely new conceptual platform for a reappraisal and a reinterpretation of all biological systems, from viruses and bacteria to man. The intellectual impact has been no less than the influence of Darwin's view of evolution through natural selection in the previous century, while the extension and application of genetic engineering may be of deeper and more wide-spread significance for the future of the human species. Even the most modest historian—and anyone who deals with evolution is a historian of sorts—cannot fail to sense the importance and ramifications of these discoveries.

Our present understanding of the basic role of DNA is largely confined to matters of organic inheritance, development, and evolution. But, as has been pointed out, the human species has a dual ancestry: a biparental inheritance via sexual reproduction with DNA, transmitted in the form of chromosomes by egg and sperm, as the source of coded information brought into expression initially by the processes of transcription and translation, and later by the processes of growth and development at more complex levels of organization, and a cultural inheritance of multiparental (i.e., social) origin which is acquired by a more active and personal process of learning during and after development. Human beings are not unique in having dual inheritances; any animal capable of learning acquires information through experience, but what does make human beings unique is the degree to which such experiences contribute to the final fashioning of the individual. Each individual, therefore, presents a composite front to the world: a genetic phenotype of uniqueness which is a reflection of the quality of his DNA expressed in a particular physical environment, and a cultural phenotype, which is a reflection both of the genetic phenotype (i.e., much behavior is probably genetically determined) and of the social environment within which the individual has his being. The biology and culture of the human species can scarcely be considered unrelated to each other, but the relative contributions of nature (biology) and nurture (culture) to the phenotypic expression of an individual have not been satisfactorily resolved. The result is that the dichotomy as well as the unity of man continues to be emphasized, the former often in narrowly religious, political, and educational, as well as anthropological, terms. But no human individual can be adequately defined or delineated in terms of one or the other of these two forms of inheritance.

Both systems of inheritance are information-based, and both operate in a dynamic environment. Further, there is no reasonable scientific ground for disagreeing with the idea that cultural inheritance and evolution were formative influences of enormous adaptive significance to the human species as it evolved from a primate stock. To believe otherwise is to deny the relevancy of a scientific approach in trying to understand ourselves. A number of questions, however, clearly await unequivocal answers. How are these two forms of evolution related to each other? What are the respective informational bases of the two evolving systems? How is information in each system transformed from a latent to an actual state of expression? Are the two systems sufficiently similar to allow a logical and meaningful comparison to be made without distorting the evidence beyond reasonable limits, and without doing scientific injustice to either system? Or can comparisons be made only by analogy, making thereby, as some scholars have maintained, any comparisons of questionable value? These are not new questions, although each questioner seems to have framed them differently and to have given different weights to similar pieces of information. In addition to having been explored by the authors previously mentioned, these same questions, variously put, have also been touched upon by Dawkins (1976), Johanson and Edey (1981), Leakey and Lewin (1977), Sagan (1977), Tanner (1981), and E. O. Wilson (1975, 1978, 1981). Each approach provides a possible thread of substance that, in the hands of some future synthesizer, may lead us to an understanding of the whole pattern of human evolution. In the meantime we continue to sift, reject, reassemble, and give different emphases to the evidence we have.

Definitions and rationale

To avoid misunderstanding and to clarify the position from which this discussion will proceed, a number of definitions and possible justifications are needed.

A meaningful comparison between the two kinds of evolutionary change that, in complementary fashion, have brought the human species into existence, makes it essential to determine whether elements exist that play comparable roles in the two systems; whether these elements are sufficiently tangible, concrete, and of lasting duration for them to be clearly identified; and whether they are of such a nature and exhibit such a behavior that they can be discussed and compared within a single frame of reference. Such an attempt carries with it the obligation "to provide an orderly sequence of structures and systems based on principles that operate at all times and places" (Stewart 1960). It is the contention here that evolution in its several forms follows certain basic rules. To play the game of evolution, continued persistence (survival) is absolutely necessary, and this also implies the existence of some kind of replicative procedure; each evolving system must be able to tap the environment for substance, energy, and/or ideas, and then convert them into a form appropriate to itself; variation and time are required, even though the evolving elements in different systems may be different in character and expression, singly or collectively; pressure of some sort, external to these evolving elements, must be present to force the evolving system to follow a given and discernible direction, otherwise only chaos would be detectable. Our intention, therefore, is to compare elements that perform similar roles in organic and cultural evolution even if their basic and expressed characteristics are totally different. To do this requires that organic and cultural evolutionary systems be lifted out of their human matrix so that each can be examined as a separate entity, and as minutely and as definitively as its elements permit.

The use of analogy

As was pointed out earlier, a number of biologists and anthropologists have intimated that organic and cultural evolution are only analogous to each other and, as a consequence, have warned that a detailed analysis can yield little of scientific significance. Their arguments suggest, in the words of one author, that analogies are comparable to eating soup with a fork, messy and lacking in nourishment. The admonition is of dubious merit, even though one needs to recognize that the use of analogy may express uncertainty on the part of the user, with the uncertainty being ideological or linguistic, or both. Avoiding analogy, however, could dampen or block inquiry rather than open up areas of related and parallel interest and would tend, furthermore, to deny the value of information so derived, when the use of analogy may be one of the few avenues left for comparative purposes. It might be useful to recall a period in the seventeenth century when the nature of fossils was a subject of heated debate, both scientific and ecclesiastic. It was Robert Hooke, the microscopist, then secretary of the Royal Society of London, who suggested that fossils were analogous to old coins unearthed from archeological digs and that they might provide clues to the history of a people who no longer existed. The usefulness and correctness of Hooke's analogy is known to every scientist and historian. The only real question of importance is whether the use of analogy serves its purpose well or ill. Cannon (1939) argued long ago that analogy serves a purpose in providing "new insights as to the workings of parallel systems," a position more recently set forth by Pribram (1980). Gerard (1961) stated more bluntly that "we might as well accept thinking by analogy because that is the way we think, that is the way the brain is made." Analogy will be avoided when other means for a more direct comparison are at hand but will be used when necessary to examine cultural evolution in the light of the far more extensive and certain information relating to organic evolution.

Evolutionary perspective

Evolution is here defined as cumulative change occurring through time, and with sufficient direction for it to be detected as other than random fluctuations. As the Swedish biochemist

G. Ehrensvärd (1962) has said, everything in the universe "is to be itself for a short period, and then to become something else." At any moment in time the current state of an evolving system is, therefore, the result of a shift from a previous state. The shift may have occurred gradually by a constant pressure brought to bear on a system, e.g., the effect of gravitational forces on large cosmic systems through extended periods of time; or the shift may have been as geologically abrupt as the extinction of so many species in the Permian period, of the great mammals in the late Pleistocene epoch of North America, or of so many species through the action of man in our own time. The origin of new species usually takes place over many millennia, but a distinctly different culture may make its appearance within the generation time of the human species, and interspecific hybridization, coupled with polyploidy, can create a new plant species overnight. But all systems that evolve do so because of instabilities, inherent within themselves or imposed from without. In the organic and cultural realm, extinction occurs because of a failure to adapt to a particular set of circumstances; in things cosmic and chemical, extinction results from a failure to achieve a degree of stability even while undergoing change.

No predetermined direction of the evolutionary process is assumed since the basic events that underlie evolution are unique and unpredictable. Evolution can and does occur at many levels of organization, and it can affect many things and events, from the trivial to the profound, from the micro- to the macrocosmos. Every level has its own peculiarities of variable elements, rates, constraints, accidents, and responses to impinging forces. Since evolution operates within the parameters of time, however long or short the intervals, it is a historical process, and as with any other kind of history, a reasonable understanding of it depends upon the availability of information and ideas ordered into time sequences that link the past with the present.

Under the rubric of general evolution, four major levels of change are recognized: cosmic, chemical, organic or biological,

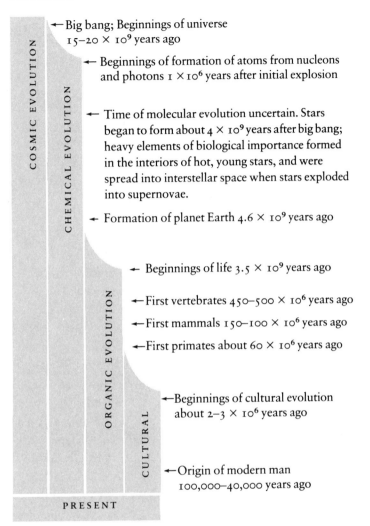

← Big bang; Beginnings of universe
15–20 × 10⁹ years ago

← Beginnings of formation of atoms from nucleons
and photons 1 × 10⁶ years after initial explosion

← Time of molecular evolution uncertain. Stars
began to form about 4 × 10⁹ years after big bang;
heavy elements of biological importance formed
in the interiors of hot, young stars, and were
spread into interstellar space when stars exploded
into supernovae.

← Formation of planet Earth 4.6 × 10⁹ years ago

← Beginnings of life 3.5 × 10⁹ years ago

← First vertebrates 450–500 × 10⁶ years ago

← First mammals 150–100 × 10⁶ years ago

← First primates about 60 × 10⁶ years ago

← Beginnings of cultural evolution
about 2–3 × 10⁶ years ago

← Origin of modern man
100,000–40,000 years ago

COSMIC EVOLUTION

CHEMICAL EVOLUTION

ORGANIC EVOLUTION

CULTURAL

PRESENT

FIGURE 3

The major types of evolution and their relation to each other. Each subsequent type arises from a predecessor system, with the branch points (dotted lines) coming into existence when a portion of the predecessor system becomes sufficiently different in complexity and responsiveness so that a new direction of change becomes established, and qualitatively different expressions are made manifest. The time scale is not proportionally accurate. The scheme depicted is comparable to the vertically branching tree of organic evolution but is to be read from top to bottom (based in part on information derived from Barrow and Silk 1980).

and cultural. While each continues on at the present time, each made its appearance in the order given, with each subsequent one emerging because of circumstances that arose in its immediately preceding system. As the number of evolving components and possible states of a system—inanimate or animate—increases, so too will there be an increase in the diversity within the system, as well as the possibilities of interactions occurring between these diverse elements. But at all times and in all circumstances, the basic rules of evolution do not change, even though the elements and processes involved may. Thus, in all systems subject to change, and independent of the degree of complexity of any given system, there will be an inevitable tendency—a selection, if you will—to move the system in the direction of equilibrium, or toward a steady state appropriate for the environment in which it happens to find itself. In the human realm, this involves the continuous reordering of phenomena in an effort to avoid a random or chaotic state (Bennett 1976), although chaos may be deliberately invoked as a step toward a new and different equilibrium. As more and more stable states are selected for and make their appearance, less stable states within the same system tend to disappear, making the system more and more resistant to forces acting on it to induce further change (Ashby 1960). The disappearance of the less stable states will have the effect of reducing diversity even as new diversities, reflecting the degree of instability, will continue to make their appearance to influence, possibly, the future state of the system. To use more familiar biological terms, and a biological frame of reference, these are adaptive processes, with selection leading toward stability, including the acquisition of more and more reliable homeostatic mechanisms (Slobodkin 1964). To paraphrase Ashby again, evolution is a series of partial successes that are retained while that which is still unstable or unsatisfactory continues to be selected. The time necessary to achieve stability depends upon the size, number, variability, and complexity of the components in any given system.

Introduction

TABLE I   *Time scale of the universe and a geological history of life forms, with numerical values to be considered approximately correct (in part from Barrow and Silk 1980).*

Cosmic time			Events	Years ago
0			Big bang	20×10^9
1 minute			Synthesis of hydrogen and helium	20×10^9
$1—2 \times 10^9$ years			Formation of galaxies	$18–19 \times 10^9$
4.1×10^9 years			First stars form	15.9×10^9
10×10^9 years			Population I stars form	10×10^9
15.4×10^9 years			Planet Earth solidifies	4.6×10^9

Geological time	Era	Period		
0	Archeozoic		Planet Earth solidifies	4.6×10^9
1.1×10^9 years		Precambrian	First forms of life	3.5×10^9
3.5×10^9 years	Paleozoic	Cambrian	First fossilized rocks of invertebrates	1.0×10^9
		Ordovician	First fishes	$5.5–4.5 \times 10^8$
		Silurian	First land planets	$4.5–4.0 \times 10^8$
		Devonian	Age of fishes first amphibians	$4.0–3.5 \times 10^8$
		Carboniferous	Age of amphibians	$3.5–2.5 \times 10^8$
		Permian	First reptiles decline of amphibians	$2.8–2.5 \times 10^8$
4.4×10^9 years	Mesozoic	Triassic	Rise of reptiles	$2.5–1.25 \times 10^8$
		Jurassic		
		Cretaceous	First mammals	$1.0–0.65 \times 10^8$
4.5×10^9 years	Cenozoic	Paleocene	First prosimians	6.5×10^7
		Oligocene	Origin of monkeys and apes	3.5×10^7
		Miocene	Origin of hominid line	$3.0–2.5 \times 10^7$
		Pliocene	Australopithecus	$5.0–0.5 \times 10^6$
		Pleistocene	*Homo erectus*	$2.0–0.2 \times 10^6$
4.6×10^9 years		Recent	*Homo sapiens*	100,000–present

17

Cosmology and evolution

The universe has evolved in a highly regular manner since the beginning of its existence about 20 billion years ago when the "big bang" occurred. In a cosmological sense, it is a homogeneous and isotropic universe in its rate of expansion and the distribution of constituent elements (Barrow and Silk 1980), but inhomogeneities have developed locally as relatively small-scale events and as the result of gravitational forces acting on, and pulling into various aggregate forms, the interstellar matter of a previously exploded universe: galaxies, islands and clusters of galaxies, nebulae, stars and star clusters, solar systems with their planetary companions, asteroids and comets. Matter itself, as atoms, formed from nucleons and photons in the very early stages of the universe, with the initial composition of the early universe consisting primarily of hydrogen mixed with a very much smaller amount of helium. As galaxies and stars were formed from gas and dust clouds by gravitational attraction, increased temperatures and pressures would lead to more random collisions, and to thermonuclear reactions which would convert hydrogen to more helium. How all the elements heavier than helium came into existence is not yet fully understood, but this evidently took place in the interiors of hot, young stars (the so-called Population I stars), rather than at the time of the original big bang (van den Bergh 1981). The explosion of these hot stars into supernovae would have distributed the heavier elements into interstellar space, after which reconsolidation could again take place. The presence and comparable proportions of heavy elements in the crust of the earth and on the moon indicate that these two bodies were formed at a different time and from different materials from those that gave birth to our sun in which hydrogen and helium predominate.

The formation of heavy elements was a necessary prelude to the beginnings of organic evolution at a very much later period of time. Life as we know it could not have originated in their absence. Carbon, oxygen, and nitrogen, in addition to hydrogen, are crucial elements in the vast array of organic molecules, magnesium in chlorophyll *a* and iron in hemoglobin are central components, while many of the elements such as zinc, copper, and manganese are essential cofactors for the proper functioning of enzymes.

According to Barrow and Silk (1980), chemical evolution involving the formation of molecules was initiated a billion or more years after the primal explosion. As the electromagnetic combining properties of atoms enabled their affinities for each other to be expressed in the form of molecules of definitive proportions and attributes, and as absorbed radiant energies heightened atomic instabilities and increased thermal reactivity, chemical aggregates of various kinds came into existence. Some would be short-lived while others, and particularly those built around carbon atoms, would be of longer duration because of their greater binding power and increased stability. The latter would increase in concentration in aqueous solution, and since there were no living forms to utilize or break them down, they tended to accumulate and to be selected for their ability to persist and, ultimately, for their capacity to increase their numbers still further through some form of replication.

Chemical evolution, therefore, arose out of cosmic evolution when an environment of appropriate conditions made its appearance. Both systems move in the direction of increased stabilities even though their arenas of action differ in scale by many orders of magnitude, and their materials, interacting forces, directions, and end products are not the same. Neither system is governed by a source of coded information but rather by physical laws governing the interaction of material bodies on macro- and microscale levels. Both systems, on the other hand, bring about increased concentrations of energy, with consequent reduction in the entropy, or randomness, of the immediate surroundings. This reduction, of course, could take place only at the expense of external sources of energy. Molecules exhibit an increased level of order, and a greater degree of complexity, as compared to their constituent atoms, and since order is itself a form of information, it can be said that the beginnings of an evolutionary trend toward a more efficient packaging of information was also becoming apparent.

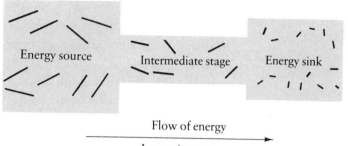

Flow of energy

Increasing entropy

FIGURE 4

The second law of thermodynamics states that open-ended systems move in the direction of degradation. Such systems require a constant input of energy if they are to be sustained through time. As table 2 indicates, various forms of energy are associated with different levels of entropy (entropy is defined as a measure of randomness or lack of order). Every evolving system makes use of external energy to sustain and drive it, orders that energy as it flows through the system, and— because no system is 100% efficient—dispels part of it into an energy sink as microwave radiation. The latter can no longer serve as a source for useful work, and therefore represents the ultimate in energy degradation. The external energy source yields energy with a lower value of entropy than that which flows through the system; some of the energy maintains the intermediate stage while the remainder passes into the energy sink as heat, or microwave radiation. Thus, in one aspect of cosmic evolution, gravitational energy, associated with zero entropy, is responsible for the formation of cosmic bodies, e.g., galaxies, stars, and planets; these are ordered systems of energy flow, with heat and other forms of radiation flowing out into interstellar space. The internal temperature of stars would have some entropy associated with it, but less than sunlight which, for example, reaches the earth and represents the external source of energy sustaining living things. The radiant energy of the visible spectrum is converted by living systems into chemical energy with a delayed entropy increase, but it serves to bring order into certain molecular structures through which life is expressed. The heat of chemical reactions in living bodies is lost to the exterior and is nonrecoverable. In cultural evolution, man's control of various energy sources has given him an adaptive advantage over all other forms of life and serves to sustain the orderliness of society, but this is accomplished only at the expense of environmental degradation (redrawn from Morowitz 1968).

Introduction

Origin of life as an offshoot of chemical evolution

Some 3.5 billion years ago life appeared as a unique and emergent phenomenon on the planet Earth. Just as chemical evolution arose out of cosmic evolution when circumstances became appropriate, so organic evolution was ushered in when aggregates of carbonaceous molecules somehow acquired that particular kind of organization and behavior we characterize as life. A process of replication would have been a significant and necessary element in the emergence of life, with some form of reproduction gradually replacing the much slower and unpredictable process of spontaneous origin. There would be an increase in the numbers of living units, and it can be presumed that these units were of sufficient stability as well as similarity to permit external forces to act on them in a selective manner. Embodied in this organization would also be a source of coded information which, through the agency of natural selection, would determine the survival and direction of change of the subsequent life forms. This would be an innovative change of enormous significance. It is the first instance of a molecule whose sole purpose was informational not only for the unit (cell) in which it was located but for future units as well.

One can imagine that initially the stability and fidelity of

TABLE 2

Forms of energy and their associated entropy values (after Dyson 1971).

Form of energy	Entropy values in arbitrary units*
gravitation	0
internal heat of stars	10^{-3}
sunlight	1
chemical reactions (including fossil fuels)	1–10
microwave radiation (heat) into space	10^4

* The higher the entropy the less likely it is that that form of energy can be used to do work.

copying the inherited information in these replicating forms would be low, but that as natural selection came into play one particular pattern of inherited information and expression would predominate. The universality of the genetic code and its mode of operation suggests that this occurred very early in the history of life.

The unpredictability of the emergence of life may be judged from the fact that the constellation of organic molecules intimately associated with life constitutes but a minute fraction of those possible. Indeed, if the recent discoveries relating to the mass of neutrinos are correct, and if neutrinos outnumber the protons, neutrons, and electrons of the universe in a ratio of a billion to one (*Science* 211 [1981]: 470–72), then the life-related molecules must be an even more infinitesimal fraction of the mass of the universe, and life as we know it may be an even more improbable event than it is presently assumed to be. This in no way denies that other forms of life are impossible, but it does indicate that the shift from inanimate to animate requires a special set of circumstances, although not a unique one. There is, for example, no particular thermodynamic reason why, from all possible states of life, the present subsets of conditions and restraints came to be selected (Morowitz 1978). There are those who would argue that when those circumstances make their appearance, the origin of life is inevitable; possibly so.

The emergent quality that constitutes life is not different, in principle at least, from the quality that characterizes water as it emerges when hydrogen and oxygen combine in an appropriate manner. Although differing enormously in complexity and expression, both life and water are examples of the appearance of an unpredictable and qualitatively new nature. However, they differ significantly from each other in that life, being based on coded information instead of invariant electrostatic forces, possesses a potential that has been so vastly exploited, and has become of such significance to us, that we have segregated it from other examples of chemical evolution and now refer to it as organic evolution.

It is clear that the emergence of these two states of being, life and water, could not have been predicted from knowledge of the properties of the components involved, emphasizing the fact that what is expressed at a simpler level is not necessarily a reliable guide to that which will be expressed at a different, and particularly at a more complex, level of organization. Each level, therefore, at which evolution will take place will express its own characteristic and innovative properties, and the manipulable units of the game will become modified even if the nature of the game is not, a point that will be stressed again when the differences between organic and cultural evolution are examined.

Jacob (1977), with a felicitous turn of words, has labeled organic evolution as a "tinkerer"; it uses what odds and ends it has available at the moment to produce a variety of systems, some of which might be workable. Those that are unworkable in the locale in which they are produced will soon disappear, and even those that do not function optimally will tend to be displaced by others that are more efficient. Some tinkering will produce neutral models which will neither improve on nor lessen the adaptability of the original prototype, although they might contribute to existing diversity which can be tapped at a later time. Environments can also change, and environmental events of greater or lesser magnitude—the Pleistocene Ice Age and great volcanic eruptions are examples—can at times wipe out whole arrays of species in indiscriminate fashion and thus affect the subsequent evolutionary scene by removing possible sources of future variation. For species that persist, however, the general trend of organic evolution has been toward greater complexity, coupled with more intricate and interlacing patterns of homeostatic mechanisms, all governed by more and more detailed and interdependent patterns of coded information.

The functions and structures of new levels of organization may differ, to varying degrees, from those of predecessor species, but their ancestry is often sufficiently discernible for us to visualize trends of change through geological time. New uses, for example, may be found for old structures. Thus, gill arches of fish may be moved forward to become transformed into primitive jaws, and the function of forelimbs may be shifted from aquatic to terrestrial to aerial motion, each shift providing the basis for a greatly changed style of existence, but the underlying structures provide the telltale details of change from one state to another. In this sense—and if we can stretch the metaphor a bit—we may think of evolution as a Picasso, creating a magnificent head of a bull by rearranging the handlebars and seat of a discarded bicycle, even while their prior functions remain readily obvious. Evolution, on the other hand, cannot be thought of as an engineer. Although there are constraints beyond which change cannot go and be viable, there are no blueprints of future models. Nor are there tools and materials to be set up in advance for the attainment of a given and predetermined end. Man may do this by invention and artificial selection, but organic evolution can be interpreted only in terms of survival in the present, not in terms of a future of uncertain character. For man to intrude into the evolutionary scene requires a well-developed sense of self and social awareness, a heightened degree of anticipation, and the ability to see one's images projected forward in time to the point of realization. But these actions are characteristic of cultural, not organic, evolution (Bennett 1976).

Organic evolution, therefore, works in the short term and opportunistically; that is, variation, when it is expressed, must coincide in time and place with an appropriate environment if it is to have a selective value and to become incorporated into the future genotype of the species (Simpson 1967). Because any change in a previously selected, closely ordered, adaptive system is more likely to be detrimental than beneficial, changes that persist are generally variation on a theme instead of genuine innovations (Stebbins 1969). In fact, the "opportunistic calculus of probabilities," as Smith (1961) expresses it, makes it far more likely that the tinkerer will produce changes of no immediate use and hence discardable, for evolution is far too parsimonious, as well as being blind, to permit organisms the luxury of retaining novelties in the hopes that they may be of future use. Among the variants in any species, preadaptation may seem to have occurred, as suggested by DDT resistance in insects or antibiotic resistance in pathogenic bacteria, but these are fortuitous, not planned, changes. Genuine innovations are therefore rare in evolution, as Stebbins insists, but even when they do occur within a species they are typically conservative in that while they do give rise to change, it is a change that cannot drastically alter the existing way of life. The reason is fairly straightforward. A species is a particular constellation of many characters, all intimately integrated with each other; drastic and innovative change would disrupt this integration. The entire mammalian group of species, including man, is testimony to such thematic variation.

Evolution as adaptation

Organic evolution, therefore, is a process operating within constraints; it is limited by that which can be tinkered with and by the environment in which species have their being. Nevertheless, analysis of individuals within particular species has revealed, in almost every instance, substantial reservoirs of heritable variations many of which are neutral in that they have no appreciable effect on the adaptability of the individual or the species. Others are of sufficient phenotypic effect and penetrance to respond, favorably or unfavorably, to the selective action of the environment. A glance at the faces at a cocktail party would reveal many variations that probably have little or nothing to do with survival or reproductive success, while the many breeds of dogs in a kennel show, brought into existence by artificial selection, would undoubtedly fare variously if allowed to compete with each other in the wild. Biochemical studies reveal that the same spectrum of genetic differences exists at a more subtle molecular level. Given this variation, and the fact that most species reproduce to a greater extent than the environment can support, it is evident that the greater the extent of diversified niches available, and the greater the amount of time available for environmental exploration and exploitation, the greater will be the number of variants within a species that can be tested. As a consequence, the phenotype, expressed morphologically and behaviorally, becomes a means for testing genetic recipes (Bateson 1963). Every environmental challenge and every expressed variation becomes a problem which the individual or the species must face. If the challenge is of short duration and not lethal, most species have sufficient physiological flexibility to handle such stress, but if it is of a persistent nature extending over many generations, adaptation would tend to be achieved by heritable means.

Every environmental challenge and heritable variation are forms of encountered or induced chaos, and a high degree of chaos cannot be tolerated for long by any living system. The stability of the genotype is therefore as important as is the maintenance of a reservoir of variation. It would be expected, then, that a species must have some means of dampening the extent of permissible variation and of keeping the species on a relatively even structural and behavioral keel. There are a number of ways by which this kind of stability can be attained, one of which is the gradual emergence of an interlocking series of homeostatic mechanisms. These are adaptive devices, both physiologically and heritably. Just as a thermostat keeps temperature within a given range, so do the homeostatic mechanisms keep the physiological processes within appropriate ranges. They also provide a means for resisting changes in the genotype, largely because of the price exacted by any change that has an effect on the integration of the phenotype as a whole (Bateson 1963; Ashby 1960). The more complex the species in a structural and physiological sense, the more intimately coordinated these adaptive measures will be, making striking patterns of innovation less likely than additional variations on a theme.

All of this would suggest that organic evolution proceeds by the gradual accumulation of small, heritable changes. This view has come to be known as neo-Darwinism, with substantial support emerging from the genetic analysis of populations

(Huxley 1942; Dobzhansky 1970). However, this cannot be the total answer to the manner by which organic evolution operates through time. It has already been mentioned that some plant species can arise abruptly and successfully as a result of interspecific hybridization accompanied by polyploidy. The domesticated wheats, tobaccos, and cottons are probably examples of such sudden emergences, and the fact that of the species of flowering plants more than one-third are polyploid indicates that such circumstances are not uncommon.

The recent analysis of paleontological data is also pertinent in this regard. Some 230 million years ago, at the juncture of the Paleozoic and Mesozoic eras, and again at the end of the Cretaceous period, about 65 million years ago, vast assemblages of species disappeared from the fossil record through what seems to have been mass extinction. Raup (1979) estimates, on a worldwide basis, that some 96 percent of all species of all kinds must have been wiped out during the first great extinction, leaving but 4 percent to repopulate the landscape during the Triassic period. The exact figures of loss may be less severe than Raup indicates (Gould 1980), but the data leave little doubt that the course of evolution can be affected by random events unrelated to gradual natural selection. Some of these may be so small as to have no detectable effect on diversity, while others may be of the magnitude described by Raup (see also Stanley 1979, 1981).

In any event, and for all its complexities, organic evolution arose as a variant form of chemical evolution, even though we still have little understanding of why a particular organization of molecules manifested those qualities that we have come to associate with life. Some of the molecular changes assumed to be related to the emergence of life can be manipulated experimentally under simulated protolife conditions, and molecules such as nucleotides and amino acids, which are universally parts of the living system, can be so produced. There seems to be little doubt that reasonably stable and self-replicating molecules, with primitive informational content, came into being through such circumstances and represented the first step toward living forms and the initiation of evolution through natural selection, but later steps leading to the first ancestral cell, with its greater organization and informational content, remain unknown at the present time. Eventually, however, an organized structural and functional entity emerged which on a continuous basis could take in, process, and transform for its own use externally derived energy and matter; could pass this capability on, via reproductive processes, to reasonable replicas of itself; and, because of variations in its inherited source of coded information, could adapt to varying environmental circumstances through a combination of chance and the processes of natural selection. Those incapable of doing so for any protracted period of time disappeared, some to be revealed as fossils in sedimentary rock, others to pass into oblivion, leaving no evidence of their existence. Some 3 billion years or more after the initial appearance of life, another organizational and behavioral change made possible the emergence of a different form of evolution. A central factor in the creation of the human species, the phenomenon of culture made its appearance as a kind of evolving behavior that could only be exploited by a species having attained a particular form of structural modification and neural sophistication and plasticity.

The concept of culture

A detailed cross-level comparison of organic and cultural evolution will be deferred until the evolving basis of each has been explored, but if we are to deal with cultural evolution as a process of continuous change we need to establish (as we did with organic evolution) what we are discussing and the procedures by which comparisons are to be made. In making a cross-level comparison, the strictures set forth by Miller (1965) will be followed. This means that certain conditions must be met if the comparison is to be judged reasonable and of predictive value: (1) a process or a system existing at one level of organization must be suspected of having a more or less formal isomorphism or identity with that which exists at a different but related level of organization; (2) units and/or modes of operation inherent to both systems must be such that they can be identified, examined, and compared so that their degree of isomorphism can be confirmed, disproved, or dismissed as irrelevant for comparative purposes; and (3) the comparison being undertaken must have a sufficiently wide relevance to be worthy of extended consideration. The assumed commonalities shared by both organic and cultural systems suggest, at least initially, that Miller's strictures are met. The basic assumption being made is that cultural evolution is but another, albeit different, manifestation of organic evolution even as the latter, at an earlier period, was but a different manifestation of chemical evolution. More is involved than the simple recitation of analogies. Although culture, seen in retrospect, was a change of a most significant and innovative character, it nevertheless reflects its biological origins and modes of operation at the same time that it assumes a different character and, eventually, a unique and identifiable existence. Culture is both a means by which a particular species met the challenges of a changing environment as well as a reflection of the manner by which those challenges were met.

An acceptable definition of "culture" is not readily apparent because for present purposes most definitions seem limited in scope. White (1959), for example, has focused on the process of verbal symboling, i.e., language, as a uniquely identifying feature, while Lenski and Lenski (1978) limit their definition to the information conveyed by symboling. Other anthropologists discuss culture in terms of material artifacts or in terms of what these artifacts reflect of cultural attributes, but the majority couch their views variously in behavioral terms or consequences. Thus, Murdock (1960) views culture as "a system of collective habits"; Hoebel (1960) as "an integrated sum total of learned behavior traits which are manifest and shared by the members of a society"; Conrad (1964) as a "series of integrated patterns for behavior developed from mass habits"; and Campbell (1966) as a "behavioral pattern developed in a social context." It can be assumed, therefore, that culture is a learned rather than an inherited pattern of information governing certain aspects of behavior and that it is a mosaic of many features which had, not its origin, but its flowering, within the context of a social group of protohuman species. The ability to perceive, know, learn, and conceptualize is biologically conferred and is more than simply the behavioral phenotype of the human species. In evolutionary terms, culture is a highly successful adaptive strategy that has its roots buried deep in vertebrate history. Bonner (1980), for example, has defined culture very broadly and, by doing so, has extended its early beginnings far down into the animal kingdom. Thus, he defines culture as "the transfer of information by behavioral means, most particularly by the process of teaching and learning." The difficulty with this definition is not that the stirrings of culture could not have had ancient biological origins; rather it is that the definition concentrates on the processes of transfer of information instead of on the nature and origin of that which is to be transferred. Attention is, therefore, directed to what are secondary phenomena rather than to that which is primary and more fundamental.

The concept of culture as expressed by Geertz (1966) seems to be focused at a more basic level, thereby making a comparison with organic evolution more reasonable and meaningful. In his view, "cultures are best seen not as complex behavior patterns . . . but as sets of control mechanisms." These are the thermostats of culture, the homeostatic mechanisms that are a reflection of integrated cultural information, contributing in great measure to conformity and stability, without dampening the total influence of individual diversity or denying it the opportunity of modifying the cultural scene. In other words, culture arises out of the acts of experience selectively transformed and codified by a social group into a number of mental images or concepts that are capable of being expressed in some tangible social form. As someone has said, culture is human consciousness working out its plan of existence. These concepts provide each individual with a set of guidelines determining the frame of reference within which his social behavior is to be expressed. To an organism or species of increasing neural and social capacity and complexity, the input of sensory information increases in parallel fashion for the simple reason that culture itself becomes an added and complex component of the environment to which adaptation must be made. A portion of these mental concepts, when shifted from the private world of the individual to the public arena for social scrutiny, can become widely shared and possibly accepted, after which they can be transformed by repetition into habit and be expressed as a form of controlled behavior. The elements of culture are individually and privately generated but only become recognized as a part of culture when they are socially incorporated. Others of these concepts do not become widely assimilated but can be retained by one or more individuals to expand the reservoir of potential cultural diversity. At some later time or in differing circumstances, they may contribute to the variation out of which new elements or sets of order can arise.

To quote Geertz (1966) again: "undirected by cultural patterns man's behavior would be virtually ungovernable, a chaos of pointless acts and exploding emotions, his experience virtually shapeless. Thus, culture is not just an ornament of human existence, but an essential condition for it." But what is uniquely characteristic of man is his very generality and his plasticity of response to incoming messages from the environment, including those from his fellow human beings. The emergence of the human species from a protohuman base represents, therefore, something of a paradox. Recognizing that in any social context total freedom is almost the equivalent of total chaos, the development of control mechanisms that are socially held and publicly expressed (e.g., rites of passage, dietary patterns, selection of a bride, division of labor) lessens the independence of the individual as these mechanisms become more and more institutionalized by the social group. At the same time it liberates those features of the receiving sensory and responding neural systems that enable the individual to adapt to new cultural situations and to enter into relations with his fellow beings in such a manner that his human-ness is encouraged and expanded. It involves a singular duality, "the search for autonomy in the midst of constraint and the countervailing search for control in the face of license" (Bennett 1976). Or as Cannon (1939) expressed it, "with essential needs assured, the priceless unessentials could be freely sought."

Cultural evolution

As in any evolving system that prevails through protracted time, there is a balance struck between those features serving to retain it within identifiable limits and those that can vary sufficiently to permit change to take place and adaptation to occur. Culture, as a result, can be advantageously viewed as an ecological system within which internal and external adjustments are constantly being made and assessed (Butzer 1980). The parallel between a culture and a species is evident.

In somewhat different terms, culture can also be thought of as a structured and controlled ideology that provides the guidelines and sets the tone of a social group, a matrix within which a rapidly learning individual can develop into a functioning member of a social group, an ambiance within which vocal and gestural symboling becomes the primary mode of information transfer. The fact that the human species arose out of a primate line noted for its noisy vocalizing and demonstrative behavior probably made for a relatively easy transition to a more subtle and abstract form of adaptive integration as well as to a more rapid and accurate form of mass communication (Jerison 1976; Tanner 1981). As signals gradually came to be transformed into symbols, one can well imagine that the first "words" spoken by one individual to another were little better than random fragments of noise. With repetition, however, the singular noise became a bridge connecting a particular image with a particular facet of the environment, and a word was born and shared. As the late poet and sculptor Thomas McGlynn has said (McAlister 1981):

> The word conceived
> in the mind of man

　　joins man to man
　　in time's communion.

Each new environmental encounter, if useful or interesting, involved an act of interpretation and integration; sharing it also involved an act of translation as the symbol came to represent the image. In this manner a vocabulary was acquired, and the environment and the relations between individuals were symbolically manipulated. Symbols, therefore, have an informational content, but that content is dependent not only on the symbol itself but equally on the artfulness with which the symbol is used and the probability that the meaning of the symbol is received as intended (Morowitz 1978). The full and effective use of symbols evolves with time, and more so as symbols and the images they represent become linked sequentially. They become "the charter of our freedom" as human beings (Frye 1981).

　　The emphasis on context and process rather than on content and product enables us to compare on more reasonable grounds things cultural with those biological. King and Wilson (1975), for example, have compared the protein products of forty-four structural genes shared by humans and chimpanzees and have found a very high degree of correspondence of amino acid sequences. The differences are far less than those known to exist between many sibling species. A similar degree of correspondence has also been found at the level of chromosome morphology (Yunis et al. 1980), so it would appear that protein and chromosomal variations do not reflect the profound mental, behavioral, and morphological differences that separate man from the chimpanzee. To account for these limited molecular and much more obvious phenotypic differences, King and Wilson suggest that they might be attributed to variations in the patterns of regulation. The assumption here is that such variation is controlled by regulatory genes that, instead of giving rise to a protein product, govern the timing and rates of the processes of growth and development, particularly during the crucial determinative stages of embryogenesis. It is also assumed that seemingly minor variation in the genes acting at this time could lead through magnification to the manifold differences that later distinguish man from his primate relatives. A good deal more information, however, is needed to place such hypothesizing on firm experimental ground.

If, for the moment, we can anticipate the gist of the next chapter, we can think of the coded information of a culture as its sociogenotype, made up of a collection of integrated sociogenes or mental concepts and providing us with a basis for equating a culture and a species, each being representative of its own kind of information expressed in a given environment. The phenotype of a culture is, consequently, the expressed imagery of its collective self and its environment, even as the phenotype of a species is that of its gene pool in a particular ecological setting. Without a common fund of shared and expressed information, inherited or learned, individuals could not be given specific or cultural designations; on the other hand, possessed of such information each individual is representative of a species or a culture while still retaining that degree of uniqueness which is a measure of the diversity of the two gene pools.

MAN IS A VERTEBRATE, a mammal, a primate, and, finally, a human being, a member of a monotypic genus that gradually came to exist within the constraints of a uniquely complex, self-invented, and self-imposed society and culture, with all that the term *culture* implies. This is a bare-bones description, revealing little of the prior sequence of changes and events that brought the human species to its present state. Recently an upsurge of interest has led a number of authors to deal with the evolutionary pattern of organic changes that took place within the hominoid and hominid groups as it unfolded during the latter stages of the Cenozoic period; the approach here is a more general one and attempts to reach back in time to the beginnings of the vertebrate line in order to search for those trends that would, in their totality, give to the human species its shape, substance, and behavior, to round out the contours of an emerging humanness, and to seek, with as much scientific rigor as possible, the evolving bases of human culture.

An attempt to capture the essence of man has had a long history, and literary sources, sacred or otherwise, reveal how difficult it is to delineate him with clarity. Genesis tells us that man was made in the image of God, but only imperfectly so. Thus, Job, searching for his faith and his self-respect as he was being sorely tested by continuing misfortune, asks of the Lord "What is man, that thou doth make so much of him . . . and that thou should test him every morning, and try him every moment?" The Lord counters this with another question and, out of a whirlwind, asks "Where were you when I laid the foundations of the earth? Tell me if you have understanding. . . . Or who laid the corner stone thereof; when the morning stars sang together, and all the sons of God shouted with joy? . . . Wilt thou condemn me that you may be righteous?"

Hamlet, in his despair, exclaims "What a piece of work is man! how noble in reason! how infinite in faculty! . . . the paragon of animals! And yet, to me, what is this quintessence of dust?" Or, as Alexander Pope describes him in his *Essay on Man,* "The glory, jest, and riddle of the world!" Robert Louis Stevenson (1888) turned the image around and came far closer in understanding the duality that is man by describing him as "a monstrous spectre . . . the disease of an agglutinated dust . . . a thing to set children screaming . . . yet invested with that mystery that is at the heart of his humanity: the thought of duty; the thought of owing something to himself, to his neighbor, to his God; an ideal of decency to which he would rise if it were possible, a limit of shame below which, if possible, he will not stoop." One would have a sense of knowing such a man, and so much more so than the sterile, mechanical creature of Buckminster Fuller (1938): "A self-balancing, 28-jointed, adapter-based biped, an electrochemical reduction plant, integral with segregated stowages of special energy extracts in storage batteries for subsequent activation of thousands of hydraulic and pneumatic pumps with motors attached; 62,000 miles of capillaries. . . . Millions of warning signal, railroad and conveyor systems. . . . Dismissed with the appellation, Mr. Jones!"

But these descriptions, perceptive and insightful as they are, tell us little of the dual heritage of man; they tell us of his present being, not of his becoming, and they do not hint of the 3 billion or more years of trial and error in the face of an indifferent, and even hostile, environment, of the successes and compromises of existence that are encoded in the molecular struc-

ture of his genes, or of the evolutionary route taken, which, as
the poet has said, made all the difference. Nor do they tell us of
the million or more years of the recent geological past during
which man would create for himself and his tribe a new way of
life, with the elements of his culture translated symbolically
through his language, and reflected both in the governing constraints of his social organization and in the freedom he enjoys
as an individual. We need not travel the entire route, however,
for it is only when we encounter the first vertebrates that we
can, with the hindsight given us through paleontological data
and a more accurate reading of time, gain some intimations of
what happened along the way.

Early vertebrate evolution:
facing an unknown future head-on

An outburst of richly diversified species occurred as the Cambrian gave way to the Ordovician period, some 400 to 500 million years ago. The richness of the faunal evidence may have resulted from a genuine explosion of new forms, or it may have
been that the evolution of calcified or silicified tissues made
them more easily fossilized and, hence, more readily detectable. But out of this diversity appeared the first fishes, one group
of which was destined to be ancestral to a later land-based vertebrate line. These were the ostracoderms with their heavily
plated skin, which was most solidly plated over the head region
and fragmented into smaller, but articulated, plates over the
body where motion required a greater degree of flexibility. The
plates could have served one of two functions: as a defense
mechanism against predatory and carnivorous water scorpions
(the eurypterid theory of Romer [1954]), or as a physiological
device to separate the more concentrated body fluids from the
more dilute environment of their fresh-water surroundings
(Smith 1961). What was of greater consequence to the unfold-
ing drama of evolution, however, was the obvious encephalization that had taken place. The sensory receptors were being
concentrated in the head region, along with a similar concen-

tration of the neural tissues needed to receive, filter, and integrate the constant flow of messages emanating from the environment, and, subsequently, to redirect the appropriate messages to the motor centers for whatever action was necessary. We might even say, somewhat facetiously to be sure but nonetheless accurately, that man's piscine ancestors faced an uncertain future head-on. It appears that the surrounding environment was one of limited niches for occupation, being restricted to the muddy bottoms of lakes and streams. Nature rarely seems to overplay its hand, so the neural tissues that were needed to apprehend and react to this environment were limited in amount. But the mind, a product of the central nervous system, is an evolved phenomenon, and the mind of man had to have its beginnings somewhere. This seems as good a place as any for a start.

Encephalization, however important it would be for the eventual emergence of the human species, was not an evolutionary invention of the vertebrates; it had occurred well before their initial appearance in ancient waters. A vast assemblage of invertebrates (for example, the whole array of worms and arthropods) had previously become encephalized as radial symmetry gave way to bilateral symmetry. But a direct and easily followed route from invertebrate to vertebrate encephalization is not readily detectable since the nervous systems of the two groups are constructed on different plans, although not in mode of action. The emphasis placed here on encephalization, however, is that this evolutionary trend would culminate in the forward concentration of sensory elements and nervous tissues, without which culture, as defined in human terms, would never have made its appearance.

The ostracoderms themselves were not predatory. They were small fishes, not much over two inches in length and with no semblance of jaws. They were, in fact, mud-grubbers, possessing no mouth parts capable of handling large pieces of food and obviously incapable of biting. Instead, paired gill pouches served to filter food particles from the detritus on the bottoms of lakes and streams (Romer 1968). Nor did they possess the paired fins which would be the forerunners of the appendages of higher vertebrates. The torpedolike body, which was adapted for existence in and movement against running water, had been perfected in earlier chordates, but in later descendants the body would be reinforced and maintained by an internal skeleton of a bony nature: skull, backbone, and rib cage. The bony skeleton is of ancient origin, and it may well be, as Romer suggested, that the cartilaginous skeleton of present-day sharks and, possibly, lamprey eels are derivative of, rather than ancestral to, bone. Motion as well as equilibrium in the ostracoderms was maintained by vertical fins, but the paired lateral pectoral and pelvic appendages would not be evident until the jawed fishes came into existence; their initial function would be that of stabilizing rudders on a more rapidly mobile form (Romer 1954).

The early events of piscine evolution took place in a theater of fresh water, but eventually some members of the group, pushing against the constraints of their environment, invaded oceanic water to take up a new mode of existence. A vast array of forms soon evolved. If we keep in mind that it is the entire phenotype of a species—physiological, structural, and behavioral—that encounters and is acted upon by the environment, we can then appreciate the constellation of changes that came to characterize the fishes as they became the dominant forms throughout the remainder of the Paleozoic era, a duration of some 200 million years. The heavy armor of the ostracoderms was replaced by an internal skeleton covered by a naked or scaly skin; except in a few species, the internal skeleton would become ossified into bone to which the muscles were attached; paired lateral fins, developed from outpocketings of the skin, served to control the rolling motion encountered in more open waters; and the forward movement of the gill arches led to the development of articulated jaws, equipped with grasping or tearing teeth derived from modified scales moving into position. The sluggish mud-grubber was transformed into a mobile predator, with a richer diet more consistent with that of an active organism. Further, food was no longer strained from the mud but taken in as chunks; the digestive tract would have reflected this change in eating habits. Increased mobility itself, as well as an altered life style that would include defensive in addition to predatory tactics, would place an enhanced premium on the increased forward concentration of the sensory receptors and on an improvement of the responding and motor systems protected by, and anchored to, a sturdier bony skeleton. To integrate these changes into a functional whole would lead to further increase in encephalization and amount of brain per unit of body weight (Jerison 1976).

Vertebrate "halfway house": the amphibians

The conditions of the terrestrial world are different and generally harsher when compared to the more or less uniform conditions of the seas and rivers, and adapting to it would demand drastically modified sets of structures and functions. The amphibians, as their name implies, did not quite make the transition, stopping at a sort of vertebrate "halfway house"; that is, they never fully emancipated themselves from a watery environment. Nonetheless, the partial transition exacted its price; some systems underwent significant alteration while others remained essentially unchanged. The paired pectoral and pelvic fins of the fish first became the fleshy lobed fins comparable to those we see today in the lungfish and, subsequently, the articulated and bony limbs of the amphibian with their extensor and retractor muscles. The air bladder, an outpocketing of the esophagus, became the paired vascularized lungs, with the circulatory system rerouted from gills to lungs by way of a three-chambered heart. Oxygen was absorbed through the moist lining of the oral cavity, or air was gulped and forced into the lungs by oral pressure, rather than being drawn in and out by action of a diaphragm as in the higher vertebrates. The problem of desiccation was solved by the toads with the acquisition of an impervious skin; the frogs and salamanders did not make this transition. No amphibian species accommodated fully to terrestrial reproduction. They lay their fishlike eggs in water where they are fertilized by sperm shed by the male, and the fishlike larval tadpoles, with fishlike gills, live in an aquatic environment until a complete metamorphosis transforms them into a semiterrestrial adult.

Poised between land and water, leading a "double life," as it were (Romer 1954), the amphibians nonetheless constituted one of the sequent steps along the road to man. Mark Twain, in his tongue-in-cheek description of evolution, jumped from fishes to reptiles (see DeVoto 1974), but nature did not do so. In addition to the problems of adapting to a new environment, there were others that had to be solved as well if terrestrial life were to be more than just a temporary thrust into an unoccupied niche. Since the amphibians have been in existence since the Devonian period, some 300 million years ago, they have had a fair measure of success even if they are not presently a dominant element in the fauna. The ambiguous existence of the

FIGURE 5   *Brain weight as a function of body weight on a log-log scale. Living mammals (——————); archaic mammals (— — —); living reptiles (—·—·—); archaic reptiles (-----) (modified from Jerison 1976).*

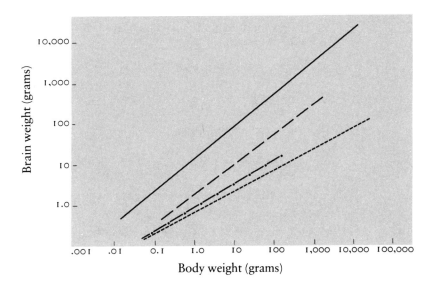

frog is reflected in its sense of sight. With a fixed-focus eye, it is near-sighted on land, far-sighted in water, but the substantial development of the optic lobes of the brain handles the integration of the stimuli flooding in from its dual environment. The disposal of nitrogenous wastes and the retention of bodily fluids had to be successfully managed. In water, poisonous ammonia resulting from the breakdown of proteins can be excreted through the gills or skin; on land this is not possible, and the amphibians reveal the evolution of an internal excretory system that solved the problem by packaging the nitrogenous wastes in the form of nonpoisonous urea, temporarily stored in a bladder, and subsequently excreted as urine. The tubules of the modified kidney served to reabsorb water in order to maintain the character of the body fluids. These features would be taken care of by homeostatic mechanisms that previously had not existed.

The paired appendages, now jointed and articulated with identifiable bones, lifted the body partially off the ground and altered the pattern of mobility. Whether jumping is an improvement over swimming, and therefore requires a more sophisticated neural circuitry to bring it off, is debatable; the relatively small (if any) increase in total brain volume (Jerison 1976) would suggest that the problems of adaptation of fish and amphibians are not significantly different in detail, although a decrease in midbrain and an increase in forebrain mass would also suggest that the problems encountered in terrestrial life required some rearrangement of neural circuitry.

The invasion of land

The reptiles, emerging out of an amphibian stock to become the dominant animal form of the Mesozoic era, broke once and for all the bondage to water. Fertilization was internal, with the probability of success much improved, and the relatively protected eggs, now fewer in number, were laid and hatched in a terrestrial, albeit moist, environment. Romer (1954) has called this evolutionary change "the triumph of the egg," the "most marvelous single invention in the whole history of vertebrate life." The egg, as he pointed out, was "a substitute for the amphibian's natal pond," an encapsulated swimming pool protected by an outer durable shell, covered with a richly vascularized membrane through which gases could be exchanged, provided with an embryonic bladder for the temporary storage of wastes, and fitted with a food supply (yolk) and a liquid-filled sac within which the embryo could develop. The hatched reptile was a miniature edition of the adult, relatively able to fend for itself. A variable amount of parental care, depending on the species, was invested in the fate of the offspring, a factor that has a bearing on the number of eggs that must be laid in order that there be a sufficient number of adults to continue the species. The relation of egg number to reproductive and evolutionary success in one reptile, the green turtle, has been most imaginatively dealt with by Carr (1967).

Reptilian mobility would be much improved over that characteristic of the amphibians by getting the body up off the ground, although most reptiles still possess a sprawling stance; the body is slung between the legs, with the legs attached laterally to the sides of the body rather than being beneath the body, as in the more mobile mammals. Some of the Mesozoic dinosaurs achieved bipedalism, with presumably greater mobility, but none have persisted. Increased mobility spawns its own problems. The environment becomes more complex as horizons are broadened, and the flow of incoming sensory stimuli increases in frequency as well as in diversity. If a prey-predator relationship is involved, signals from a distance as well as from nearby sources must be received, and the relevant signals must be distinguished from background noise so that appropriate assessments and decisions can be quickly made. Survival is often dependent upon the correct decision made on the basis of partial evidence, so the mechanisms favoring selective, integrative, and interpretive success would become more reliable with time and practice and would be gradually reinforced by genotypic changes. It is perhaps axiomatic that a complex environment can be perceived and handled only by a complex organism, one equipped with improved sensory and motor capabilities, and a brain capable of integrating rapidly received, diverse information. This would suggest the need for a brain mass relatively larger per unit of body size, but Jerison (1976) states that the adaptive radiation of the reptiles into a broad spectrum of environmental niches seems to have accomplished without any significant increase in brain size. It would appear, therefore, that fishes, amphibians, and reptiles needed but minor increases in neural mass to perfect and accomplish their adaptive tactics, but this is probably an oversimplification of the situation since there is a gradual and relative reduction in midbrain mass correlated with a parallel increase in the forebrain as evolution proceeds from fishes to reptiles. It should be realized, however, that these changes were occurring in a brain of small dimensions. For example, the stegosaur, a dinosaur of elephantine size, had a brain about the size of a walnut. What is most likely to have happened is that a gradual shift occurred with sensory input and motor output moving from midbrain to forebrain, the latter being that area that, in the mammals, would be generally concerned with association and integration of information.

FIGURE 6

Comparison of reptilian and mammalian posture. In the former the body is hung between the limbs, a stable but energy-consuming posture: mobility is limited. In mammals the body weight is thrust through the long bones, which gives greater mobility although a more unstable stance. Mobility brings on its own set of problems because the central nervous system as well as the sense organs must adapt to a more rapidly changing world.

The emergence of the mammals

The reptiles were an amazingly successful and diverse group of species, dominating the 125 million years of the Mesozoic era and invading, as they did, terrestrial, aerial, and watery niches. Their dietary habits were broadly diverse, and their ranks included herbivores, carnivores, and insect eaters; their size range was enormous, from the huge dinosaurs to those as small as chickens; they were nocturnal as well as diurnal; and they achieved bipedalism long before man made his appearance. Why they, and especially the dinosaurs, declined toward the end of the Cretaceous period has been endlessly debated without resolution, but one group would become the progenitors of the mammals. These were the therapsids, a nocturnal, mammallike assemblage of species which split off from the main reptilian line soon after its emergence from an amphibian stock and which were eventually displaced by the larger diurnal dinosaurs. Before their demise, however, they gave rise to the insectivores, the most primitive of the mammalian group, whose present-day relatives include the mole and the several kinds of shrews. The earliest mammals, therefore, coexisted with the dinosaurs during their long period of Mesozoic dominance and gave little evidence of their evolutionary potential until they were able to invade the ecological niches left open by the declining dinosaurs. They were the rats and mice of the Mesozoic (Romer 1954), described by Berrill (1955) as nocturnal skulkers in the underworld of leaves and rotting vegetation, incessantly active and, like today's shrews, voraciously consuming whatever crossed their paths as they burned out their brief and precarious lives. A high caloric intake was needed to maintain a high metabolic rate, which in turn was needed to offset the high loss of energy in the form of heat from their small bodies. Their dominant senses were hearing and smell as, snout first, they probed their world of darkness. These senses are forebrain related in contrast to the midbrain related and primary visual sense of the reptiles; this shift in sensory centers had much to do with the enlargement of the forebrain, as we shall discuss later.

The brain-body problem

These nocturnal insectivores exhibited a fourfold increase in relative brain size over their reptilian progenitors, thus establishing a different brain-body size ratio that would be maintained for about 100 million years. Jerison (1976) suggests that such stability indicates the successful occupation of a new environmental niche, with the niche itself undergoing little change during this period. They would remain nocturnal members of the faunal world until the end of the Mesozoic era, after which they would move into the sunlit world left unoccupied as the dinosaurs declined. The great expansion and establishment of the mammalian lines, with a pronounced tendency toward an increased body size in many of the evolving groups, took place in the Paleocene and early Eocene, about 50 to 60 million years ago. During this time an additional fourfold increase in relative brain size occurred, with the new increase in neural tissue being primarily in the forebrain. Vision once again became the domi-

FIGURE 7　*Diagrams (not drawn to scale) of the brains of a fish, amphibian, reptile, and mammal to indicate the relative size of the cerebral cortex (forebrain) with respect to other regions of the central nervous system. The cerebral cortex is stippled, with the mid- and hind-brain lying behind it and indicated in outline form. The olfactory lobes, or bulbs, are situated at the front of the cerebral cortex.*

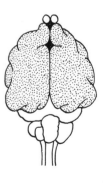

Fish　　　Amphibian　　　Reptile　　　Mammal

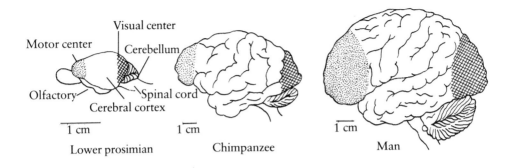

Motor center
Visual center
Cerebellum
Olfactory
Spinal cord
Cerebral cortex
1 cm
1 cm
1 cm
Lower prosimian   Chimpanzee   Man

FIGURE 8   *The changing organization of the brain, as well as increasing size as primate evolution proceeded from the lower prosimians to man. The body/brain ratio of the prosimians would be greater than that of other mammals, and the several specialized centers of the brain would reflect the life style of the organism; that is, the olfactory centers in the prosimians would diminish in relative importance as the visual sense became dominant, while the visual center would correspondingly increase in size. The motor centers would also increase in size as bipedalism, manipulable hands, and speech contributed to the more complex behavior of the higher primates, and particularly of man, while the more intricate folds of the cerebral cortex increase as learning, conceptualization, and storage of information play more and more important roles as evolution proceeds.*

nant sense, but now the visual centers were located in the forebrain, with the midbrain becoming diminished in size and relative importance.

Increasing brain size, particularly that involving the forebrain, is generally correlated with increasing intelligence, that is, with the ability to learn and to profit from experience. This is very probably so, but there is also reason for believing that increased intelligence is the result, rather than the cause, of an enlarged central nervous system. An altered life style with different patterns of sensory dominance is far more likely to be the basic cause. The first major increase in brain size occurred as the mammals split off from the primitive reptilian stock to enter a nocturnal world. In such an environment, the senses of hearing and smell became dominant, and, in order to acquire an ability to adapt to the dark, the visual system shifted its structural elements so that rods largely replaced the cone cells in the retina. Visual accommodation can take place at the retinal level by changes in the proportion, placement, and numbers of rods and cones, and in the neural network posterior to the retina that assists in the analysis of visual information. A good deal of discrimination, therefore, takes place before the visual stimuli reach the level of the brain, and relatively little increase in neural tissue would be required to meet altered visual needs. This is not so for the senses of hearing and smell. As Jerison (1976) points out, these replaced vision as the distance senses, and there had to be an increase in and a repackaging of the neural elements if these adaptive requirements were to be fulfilled. In vertebrate systems, the elements for the analysis of auditory and olfactory stimuli are in the brain proper, and an increased need for analytical ability is met by an increase in forebrain tissue rather than by a rearrangement of or by an increase in the number of sensory elements at the receptive level of the ear or nose.

The second fourfold increase in brain tissue occurred when the mammals in general left their nocturnal world to become diurnal creatures. Vision would once again become the dominant as well as the distance sense, but now the integrative centers would be located in the forebrain rather than in the midbrain, and the cerebral cortex would reflect this change in life style by an enlargement of the optic lobes.

Mammalian adaptive strategies

The two increases in neural mass, together with the more intricate neural network that accompanies such enlargement, created a new reality for each of the developing mammalian lines. Reality, of course, is defined and limited by our perceptions, and these in turn are determined by the sensory and neural elements that receive, select, and process all incoming information in the form of appropriate stimuli. Each species, therefore, creates its own reality, and each addition to the mass and intricacies of the sense organs and neural network will, by positive feedback mechanisms, alter and increase the complexity of that reality. In every way that an environment can be dissected, and in every way that environmental information can be assimilated, analyzed, integrated, and acted upon, the mammals represented an evolutionary improvement over the reptiles. Postural changes led to increased and more energy-efficient mobility as the legs were shifted from lateral to ventral positions. Sensory perception was enhanced by the development of color vision. A varied dentition reflected a diet that varied enormously from one group of mammals to another. Warm-bloodedness, a possible carryover from a reptilian group, was coupled with an increased oxygen-carrying capacity and an improved circulatory system to provide independence from ambient temperatures; this change from cold-bloodedness was not achieved without cost, however, for the maintenance of a steady temperature requires a higher and more constant fuel consumption. Reproductive strategies shifted from an external laying of eggs and little or no parental investment of time and energy in caring for the many offspring, to placental births, supplemented with a prolonged postnatal care and feeding of a limited number of offspring. An increase in neural tissue would handle in a more efficient manner the mass of information that constantly bombarded the individual. And finally, more and more sophisticated homeostatic mechanisms, based on intimately integrated neural and hormonal receptors and effectors, would evolve to take over and control the routine functions of the mammalian body, at rest and under stress. As indicated earlier, the more complicated the animal, physiologically and behaviorally, the more complex will be the environment that it perceives, and the more necessary and closely regulated will be the homeostatic mechanisms (Ashby 1960).

Primate strategies

The mammals, as a result, exhibited intelligent activity in addition to being poised and ready for action at all times (Romer

1954). The mammals underwent expansive and adaptive radiation in the early part of the Cenozoic, with one branch leading to the prosimians, the most primitive members of the order Primates. It was once assumed that the tree shrew was the ancestral form of all primates, but this concept is now generally discredited (Luckett 1980). But whatever the prosimian ancestor, evolution brought about a shift from a terrestrial to an arboreal sphere, from a nocturnal to a daylight existence, and from a primary dependence on olfactory and auditory stimuli to those of an optical and tactile character. The reptilian vision, a midbrain-governed sense, had gradually diminished in dominance in the nocturnal insectivores and was not recovered in the same form when a daylight existence was achieved once again; evolution does not appear to reverse itself to recover selectively that which has been lost. Rather, the visual circuitry came to a focus in the forebrain, as did that related to the tactile sense, with the result that the cerebrum underwent a still further increase in size.

The arboreal world, if indeed this was a part of the pathway leading to man (an arguable point of view), is a different world from that at ground level and requires different sets of qualifications if survival is to be assured. The need for a more detailed and three-dimensional perception to insure a better judgment of distances would place a greater reliance on the visual sense, while movement in an unstable aerial environment would favor an enhanced tactile sense and a heightened awareness of equilibrium. A faulty leap in such an environment would be likely to remove some genes from the breeding pool of the species. A survey of the prosimians—lemurs, tarsiers, and lorids—reveals some of the phenotypic changes that appeared with time: the face became flatter as the snout was foreshortened, and the eyes were moved from a lateral to a more forward position to provide stereoscopic vision as the images from both eyes overlapped and were integrated as one. An additional premium was also given to dexterity and muscular coordination. The terrestrially important clawed foot became the clinging, grasping, sensitively tactile, nailed organ of the arboreal primate, with the forelimbs and hands becoming highly versatile for movement, for examining and sensing the nature of objects, for grooming itself and others, and for feeding the now foreshortened face. Of necessity the brain must be appropriate to its task; it responds to or reflects the manner in which the inner and outer worlds of the species interact with each other, and it becomes, therefore, a measure of the world as it is perceived and managed.

A pattern of reproductive frugality can be found in most of the mammalian groups, but it reaches its full expression among the primates. Imagine, if you will, the difficulties of trying to feed and bring to reproductive maturity a litter of demanding offspring among the branches of a tree. Only the opossums seem to do this with success. The loss of young would probably be very high, but among the primates the pattern of reduced numbers of offspring is characteristic of terrestrial as well as arboreal species. The extant primates, with a very few exceptions (such as the marmosets), and very probably those of the past as well, bear their offspring singly; the offspring are relatively helpless and are more so the more advanced the primate species. Thus, as one passes from the prosimians to the Old World monkeys, to the anthropoid apes such as the chimpanzee, one encounters a lengthening of the period of gestation and a corresponding lengthening of the periods of infancy and adolescence, and a postponement of the attainment of adult independence, all of which is related to an increase in parental care (Lovejoy 1981). As a result, the amount and duration of parental investment becomes a significant form of behavior around which the family structure has its origins within the larger confines of a more extensive social grouping. The supreme importance of prolonged filial dependency as a necessary prelude to cultural acceptance and enhancement can scarcely be overstressed because it provided a lengthening period of learned experience to take the place of, and offset, a gradually diminishing repertoire of instinctual behaviors. The major source and development of behavioral patterns was passed, therefore, from the inherited genotype to the acquired environment, with

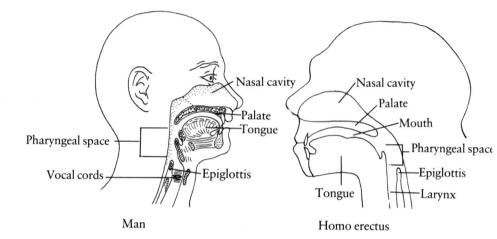

Nasal cavity

Palate
Tongue

Pharyngeal space

Vocal cords

Epiglottis

Man

Nasal cavity

Palate

Mouth

Pharyngeal space

Epiglottis

Tongue

Larynx

Homo erectus

FIGURE 9   *The vocal anatomy of H. sapiens, H. erectus, a newborn human baby, and a chimpanzee, and how the several elements affect the production of speech. Of particular importance, according to Howells (1973), are the angulation between the oral cavity and the pharyngeal space, the greater length in man of the pharyngeal space, and the position of the tongue in relation to other features of the speech tract. The nuances of speech in modern man are based on the vowel sounds produced deep in the throat where the larynx and the vocal cords are located; also the tongue extends back into the throat, where it modulates the reso-nances of vowel sounds. The consonants, on the other hand, are pro-duced in and around the oral cavity, with the lips and tongue varying its shape and size. The nasal cavity as well as the oral cavity aid in gov-erning the sounds and articulation of speech. In adult chimpanzees and newborn humans the pharyngeal space is short, with the larynx high in a curving throat and the tongue mostly located in the mouth area where it can alter only the dimensions of the oral cavity but can-not act effectively on sounds produced by the larynx. As the brain of the newborn child develops, a change in the position of the tongue and larynx occurs, enlarging the pharyngeal space and providing the anat-omy for handling an increasing repertoire of sounds. It is believed that the anatomy of H. erectus was more nearly like that of chimpanzees; if so, it must have had a form of speech in which the sounds were not well articulated (redrawn and modified from Howells [1973], and White and Brown [1973]).*

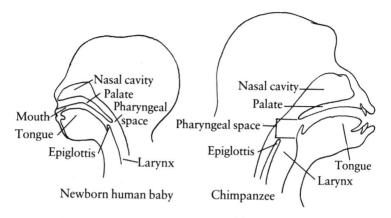

Newborn human baby   Chimpanzee

the environment for the developing offspring being largely biological and social rather than physical. Survival of the young improved significantly, and sibling interrelationships were similarly extended as periods of parental dependency overlapped within the family. Under such circumstances, the ability to learn, and to pass on that which was learned, would take on a high selective value as the social pressures increased.

Restructuring the primate

The advent of the human species from an anthropoid base was characterized, therefore, by very greatly altered structural and behavioral features. It is difficult to ascertain how much of this structural change might possibly be attributed to earlier arboreal influences and how much to other environmental and social pressures. Certainly no single feature can be judged wholly responsible, although bipedalism, while obviously structural, would be associated with behavioral changes as well. Today only a few of the primate species have a terrestrial existence. The baboon and its gaily fore-and-aft-decorated cousin, the mandrill, are ground dwellers, but man's closest relatives, the chimpanzee and the gorilla, are terrestrial only on occasion, when their mode of locomotion is basically quadripedal, with only intermittent and brief periods of bipedalism. The line leading to the human species alone acquired full bipedalism, the beginnings of it probably extending as far as the late Miocene, some 10 to 6 million years ago, and well before any semblance of a material culture in the form of tools can be recognized. Bipedalism as a way of life is not simply getting up on one's hind legs and striding into some uncertain primate future; a whole host of changes must accompany these actions, and they hardly could have occurred one by one within the presumed time span. It is the pattern of existence upon which selection acts, for the species must be in tune with its environment at all times if it is to survive. Some of the changes that accompanied bipedalism are obvious: the spine curved into a modified S-shape so that the thrust of weight of the enlarging body could pass down through an appropriately tilted pelvis and the long bones of the legs; the double-arched foot and locked knee developed to make standing a stable, untiring posi-

FIGURE 10 *Increasing brain size in a chimpanzee (upper curve) and a human child (lower curve) during the early years of growth. The chimpanzee starts off with a relatively greater brain size (although not in absolute values) and has a head start behaviorally: at the age of one year, a chimpanzee has the mental capacity of a year-old child, but the motor skills of a four year old, and the strength of an eight year old. But its adult mental capabilities do not exceed those of a human five year old, while the brain size, sexual and physical maturity, and learning capabilities of a child continue to grow and develop for a far longer period of time (White and Brown 1973).*

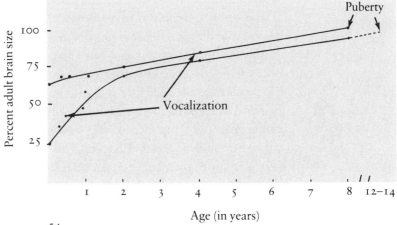

tion at the same time that altered muscle insertions permitted the flat-footed shuffle of the ape to be replaced by a more energy-efficient stride; the head, positioned on top of the spinal column, gave a better balance and a forward-looking stance at the same time that an important distance as well as a near-at-hand vision was developed; and a flattened rib cage, with the forelimbs pushed to the sides of the body by the collarbone acting as a spreader and terminated with hands fitted with opposable thumbs. A by-product of bipedalism and a shift in the position of the head would be an enlargement and a dropping down of the larynx. This, together with the coordinated movement of the tongue and lips, enabled the emerging hominid to handle the nuances of sound and eventually of language in a more flexible and innovative manner and thus paved the way for the eventual emergence of a symbolic language in order to reify his images of the world about him. There is no question about it; bone for bone, muscle for muscle, organ for organ, and even a great deal of his biochemistry as well, man retains evidence of his primate ancestry, but a tinkering evolution has rearranged and modified it sufficiently to bring a new species into existence. This early ancestor of ours walked, it did not shuffle, toward its human destiny.

Neoteny and parenting

More needs to be said about infant dependence and increased parental investment. However important altered structure and behavior might be in speciation, of at least equal importance (which is greater or lesser in importance is meaningless since all are interrelated and integrated) is the innovative change that occurred in primate ontogeny. As Gould (1977, fig. 61) indicates, there is a slowing down of the growth rate of the human embryo by a prolongation of early development stages such that the adult human individual exhibits characteristics that are more typically those of a juvenile higher primate such as a chimpanzee. Developmentalists refer to this as the phenomenon of *neoteny*. It represents a shift in the timing or regulation

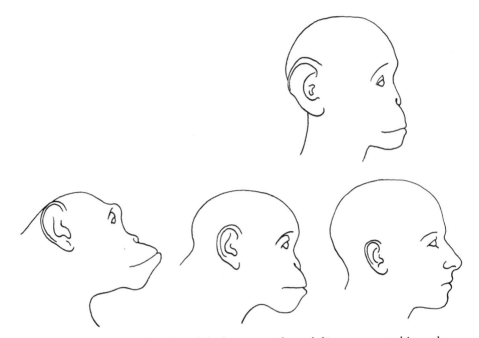

FIGURE 11   *Profiles of an adult chimpanzee (lower left), reconstructed* Australopithecus africanus *(lower center), and* H. sapiens *(female, lower right)
so that they may be compared with the profile of a very young chimpanzee (above). Except for the more prominent nose in* H. sapiens, *the
facial features of a human being are more those of the infant chimpanzee than of the adult. The reconstructed* A. africanus *indicated that
neotenization had already set in at least several million years ago (infant chimpanzee redrawn from Naef 1926; consult Gould 1977, as
well).*

of growth (the heterochrony of Gould 1977), which leads to an
alteration in the synchrony of the previous and more usual
primate developmental pattern. The speculation of King and
Wilson (1975) is of interest in this regard. After demonstrating
a high level of correspondence in the polypeptides of the chimpanzee and man, they have suggested that the morphological,
behavioral, and developmental differences between the two
species might be due to differences in the regulatory genes and
their time of action, rather than in those coding for the proteins. A somewhat similar concept has been offered by P. J.
Wilson (1980) to the effect that evolution in the primate line

has been progressively in the direction of increasing generalization of morphology. It is questionable, however, whether this concept should include the central nervous system. Throughout primate evolution there has been a steady, even a spectacular, improvement in information-processing and problem-solving abilities. This has lessened the selective pressure for morphological specializations required to perform those special tasks needed for survival, but the central nervous system represents specialization of another sort which evinces its phenotypic expression through the flexibility with which problems arising out of environmental confrontation are solved. Options instead of fixed responses emerge, and as P. J. Wilson observes, "purposeful action and thinking" become "both possible and necessary." A behavioral plasticity, therefore, becomes more evident as the constraints of instinctual channeling and the needs for specialization relax and are replaced by a period of protracted and dependent learning, which becomes extended well beyond that found in other species.

It is this period and pattern of growth and training that enabled the human species to cross the threshold separating the protocultural from the eucultural stage and, according to Lumsden and Wilson (1981), to generate "a sustained autocatalytic reaction in which genetic and cultural evolution drove each other forward." It is also the period in which these authors propose the fixation of their "epigenetic rules of mental development," rules that are involved in the automatic processing of sensory perceptions, and that subsequently are engaged in "the channeling of memory, emotional response [and] decision making." At the present time it seems best to regard the above statements as interesting and highly provocative pieces of speculation that have yet to be fully established and applied with certainty and profit.

We are all familiar with the results of neotenous development: the helpless nakedness of the human infant equipped with the barest minimum of instinctual responses; the flat face retained into adulthood instead of the thrust-out jaw and overhanging browridges of the anthropoid ape; the smaller teeth,

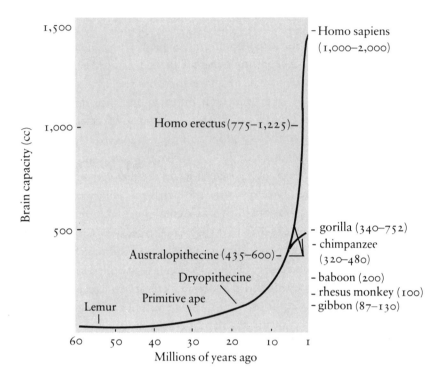

FIGURE 12 *Increasing cranial capacity during the course of primate evolution, with arrows indicating the approximate time in the past when the several forms made their first appearance (see also fig. 13). Average cranial capacities of several present-day monkeys and apes are indicated on the right, with the range in size in parentheses (modified from Swanson 1973, numerical values from Campbell 1966).*

particularly canines, and rounded arch of the jaws retained throughout life; and a continued growth of a brain following birth that results in a mass well beyond the brain/body ratio typical of other species, including other primates. The brain of man, for example, is only 23 percent of its final size at birth, so that it completes its growth to adult size during a period when parental investment in the well-being and molding of its offspring is at its most intense, when learning is readily absorbed and retained, and when behavior can be most readily manipulated by an authority figure.

The problem of brain size

The present brain capacity of adult man appears to have been reached about 250,000 years ago. Prior to that time, and during the preceding 2 or 3 million years, the brain had tripled its size as the australopithecines (400–500 cc), or some coexisting form, gave way to *Homo erectus* (ca. 1,000 cc) (or, according to some anthropologists, to *H. habilis* and then to *H. erectus*), and the latter to *H. sapiens* (1,200–1,700 cc). A survey of the anthropological literature reveals that the reasons for the great increase in brain tissue have been variously debated. Garn (1963), for example, strikes a rather general note when he suggests that the brain is a highly specialized organ of survival and that the increase in neural mass and circuitry, as well as the extensive reprogramming that has obviously taken place, can be attributed to the necessity of managing the vast amount of informational noise flooding the receptive centers of an increasingly more and more perceptive primate, and out of which relevant bits and patterns of information must be extracted for

FIGURE 13 *Comparison of the cranial capacities of the chimpanzee,* Australopithecus, H. erectus, *and* H. sapiens. *The cranium becomes more rounded as it increases in size, the face flattens as sight becomes the dominant sense, the teeth become smaller as does the lower mandible (jaw), and the brow ridges become less prominent. The arrows indicate the changing position of attachment of head to vertebral column as bipedalism is evolved.*

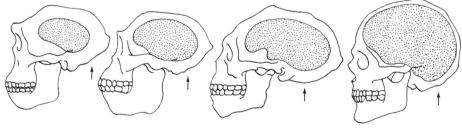

Chimpanzee
320–480 cc

Australopithecus
435–600 cc

Homo erectus
775–1,300 cc

Modern man
1,000–2,000 cc

action or storage. This, after all, is what the brain is concerned with as it processes incoming signals and attempts to handle the problems posed by an environment which now includes a high social component as well.

Other factors, however, must obviously enter in, as both Tanner (1981) and Martin (1981) point out. Martin, for example, points to the existence of a high positive correlation between brain size and metabolic rate in a stable environment, with the larger primates being more energy-efficient feeders than the smaller species. Single births allow the mother to furnish her offspring with a high-energy nutritional source during fetal development, and since this carries over into the postnatal period as well, her efficiency at the input level must be matched at the output level of nursing. Martin believes that the pattern of brain growth is established during fetal development, and in humans this must be determined by the mother's energy potential since human infants have considerably larger bodies and brains than would be suggested by the length of the gestation period. This would then account for the quadrupling of the size of the human brain in contrast with the doubling that occurs in the other primates.

Any organism is a prisoner of the information it possesses, whether that information is inherited or learned; the brain, therefore, defines and sets the limits of its universe. It can handle only those stimuli that it can absorb and process, making all else simply background "noise" that goes unrecognized and unheeded. The brain, of course, is not a substitute for experience, as Brace (1979) points out, but, equally, experience is without informational value if it fails to impress itself on, and alter the structure of, the "mind," however the mind is defined. In other words, the neural structure of a species must be consistent with its way of life, or, to put it in a reverse way, a way of life cannot transcend its neural base. We must assume, therefore, that the impetus for the rapid enlargement of the central nervous system during the Pleistocene was, in some measure, a response to an increased volume and diversity of stimuli arising out of a more and more richly varied environment. These stimuli for some reason elicited a response in one protohuman group but not in closely related forms that, at least potentially, might also have been able to respond similarly. We must further assume that the added stimuli responsible for this environmental richness were largely social rather than physical, although a move from the forested areas to the savannahs of East Africa provided a wholly new set of stimuli to be managed.

A feedback system must be involved here. Enlargement of the central nervous system means a greater number of neurons and interneuronal connections, increasing thereby the storage and integration of information and a heightened sensitivity and appreciation of the environment and its nuances. A more richly diversified existence gradually makes its appearance, this in turn placing a greater selective value on an increased capability and plasticity for the development of different and more appropriate strategies for continued adaptation. A mutually reinforcing feedback system, present in any species dependent upon the active interplay of genotypic and environmental variables, will insure a pattern of constant testing and adjustment until some extraneous, possibly unrelated, factor places limitations on further enlargement of the central nervous system. An example of this is the difficulties of pelvic accommodation to an increased cranial size at birth.

The beginnings of human culture

Thus, the earliest evidence of tool making, judged to have occurred about 2.5 million years ago, signaled the beginnings of a material culture, but some anthropologists (e.g., Lovejoy 1981; Tanner 1981) believe that a number of significant and crucial strategies for survival in a social setting had already been perfected prior to this time. In addition to those features specifically related to neotenous development (that is, to an increased maternal investment in the offspring and the enhanced opportunities for learning at an impressionable age), Lovejoy cites a lowered reproductive rate with single births widely spaced to allow for appropriate weaning; continuous sexual receptivity on the part of the female promoting continuous male proximity and, ultimately, an investment of his time in parenting; bipedalism that freed the hands for carrying provisions back to a predetermined and fixed home site and, in the process, set the stage for a division of labor within the family grouping; and a presumed increase in imaginative and integrative ability to create a more manageable and coherent world out of the chaos of received images. Lovejoy views the making of tools as a later accomplishment.

Tanner, on the other hand, focuses on the gathering of plant foods as the primary adaptation leading to a hominid status. Bipedalism, with the freeing of the hands for manipulable purposes, was critical in setting the stage for an altered way of life, but of equal importance was the shift from foraging to gathering. The former practice is nomadic in nature. Food that is

FIGURE 14

Time scales of the origin and periods of existence of the species of Australopithecus *and* Homo. *The time scales vary from one authority to another so that the ends of the periods are uncertain (indicated by dashed lines). A. afarensis, for example, may extend back in time to about 5.5×10^6 years ago. No connections between the several species have been indicated because the relationships of one species to another are not entirely clear; that is, clear-cut connecting links between species are not found or interpreted as yet, suggesting possibly a sudden origin (Stanley 1981).*

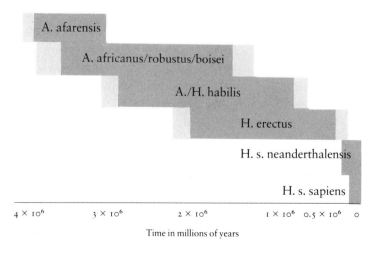

found or seized is eaten on the spot, the young are weaned as early as possible so that they can become independent foragers as well, and no fixed place of residence becomes established. Gathering may seem but a minor variation of foraging, but in actuality it involves a profound alteration in the way of life, based on a different set of conceptual images. Above all else it involves a sense of place, a place for eating, for the sharing and preparation of food, for the rearing of young in comparative safety, for the exchanging of information, and for socialization. It requires a greater knowledge of the environment and its food-producing potential in all seasons and leads in time to the invention of more efficient ways of becoming self-sustaining, including the making of tools and the perfecting of other labor-saving devices. Divisions of labor and role performance come into being. Tanner proposes that the initial step toward the fixation of such a social and cultural structure was taken by the females of the species, the benefits of which would ultimately draw in the males so that they would become a constant instead of an intermittent portion of the group. Eventually, culture would be transformed from an optional to a mandatory mode of existence, within which the human species would find its expression.

We cannot reach backward to free the Adam of symbolizers from prehistoric shadows, and there are no material evidences that tell us with certainty when a symbolic language was invented. Many would argue that the manufacture and spread of tools presuppose the existence of such a communicative device, and this may well be so, but Jerison (1976) sees the primary role of language in a different light. He argues that language, from its inception, was an adaptive means for the integration and reification of an increasing flow of sensory impressions, a way for a species of increasing intelligence, as judged from the progressive enlargement of the central nervous system, to unify and identify itself through vocal articulation. Or, to use Jerison's expression, language is "another neural contribution to the construction of mental imagery analogous to the contributions of the encephalized sensory systems and their association systems." A sense of individual and group awareness, and a growing separation of the individual from his physical environment, are implied. The result would be the closer circumscription of the social group, and a gradual redirection of its vision, inwardly to its needs and hopes and fears rather than outwardly toward nature and the ever-present problems of daily existence and survival. Under these conditions, language as a communicative means would be "a side effect to its basic role in the construction of reality" (Jerison 1976), a point of view that is in general agreement with that expressed earlier by Garn (1963). Although the behavior of man consists of both inherited and learned components, it would seem that these strategies, appearing as the Pleistocene proceeded, were more and more cultural and less and less biological in their thrust, and that as the cultural strategies became focused and refined and amplified they would come to play an increasingly significant role in the creation and definition of the species that invented them.

THREE

The Informational Bases of Evolving Systems

THE WORLD WE perceive and come to know is generally an orderly system; it is the reality with which we become familiar through exposure, observation, discovery, and, finally, understanding. The sun rises and the sun sets, and our lives are geared to its regularity; the tides move in and out on a readily perceived time schedule. Indeed, so regular is our world that predictions of many kinds can be made with accuracy: birth rates, death rates, the character of offspring from known matings, the course of a particular disease, the projected appearance of Halley's Comet many years in the future. But we are not given a ready-made model of reality; each of us constructs that reality from information that he is given and experiences to which he is exposed, and because no two individuals receive or pass through the same experiences, each of us has a unique and more or less subjective reality of his own. To the extent that we are capable of sharing our views of reality with each other, and finding that there are experiential commonalities, to that extent do realities become collectively convincing and public (Ziman 1968).

In the quartet *Burnt Norton*, T. S. Eliot said that "Human kind cannot bear very much reality," but the greater truth is that we cannot function properly without an ordered reality in which chaos is reduced to an acceptable level. As human beings, lacking most of the order which arises out of the instinctual capabilities of other vertebrate species, we need to learn to adapt to our physical and social environments, during the course of which learning we tend to impose meaning on, and give coherence to, our existence. To do so, and to gain that sense of time and place and security that is the essence of social existence, we have turned to magic, mythology, and, more recently, science to complement that which comes to us through parental and communal investment, and to create that ordered reality we require out of the piecemeal fragments of experience and existence. We have come, therefore, to recognize that whatever the source or mode of construction, there is a basic pattern of information from which any kind of social order derives its form. The pattern, differing from one culture to another, may be loosely or tightly organized, but it will inevitably reveal, on analysis, its mosaic nature. Some pieces will come from the accepted and passed-on customs, traditions, and beliefs in supernatural beings or forces, others from an imposed or accepted social authority of a more human sort. Still others will derive from a more pragmatic approach, stemming from a faith in ourselves as more or less reliable observers and interpreters of the natural scene about us, and from the nature of experiences encountered in that environment. Human nature and human existence depend, consequently, upon two very distinct and different sources of order, each based on its own unique system of information: the first is that bound up in the molecules of inheritance acquired biparentally through the mechanisms of sexual reproduction, and the second is that acquired individually and communally from the cultural and physical milieu in which we have our existence. Neither alone defines our human uniqueness, and both were required to move us from the world of animals into the world of human beings.

To what extent, if any, the epigenetic rules of Lumsden and Wilson (1981) can be invoked to aid in understanding cultural phenotypes and the basis of individual visions of reality is difficult to determine. As they point out, studies of the behavior of identical twins lend credence to their speculations on the importance of the genetic component in guiding cultural development, but the extent to which the same kind of reasoning can be applied at the learning level for those of different genetic but similar social backgrounds remains to be critically assessed.

The structure and function of DNA

The last twenty-five to thirty years of molecular and genetic studies have demonstrated beyond any reasonable doubt that the basic source of biological information, and hence of order, resides in macromolecules of deoxyribose nucleic acid (DNA), within whose structure, and in a way unique for each individual, is encoded a series of messages that are extractable and brought into expression by appropriate means and under regulated circumstances. Each source of a message is a *gene* or, for purposes that will become obvious, a *biogene*. A collection of biogenes, the number and kind varying with the species, constitutes the genotype of an individual, and their collective and orchestrated expression, the phenotype (the appearance and behavior) of that individual.

DNA is a macromolecule in the form of a double helix, consisting of two antiparallel and complementary strands of nucleotides (thymine, adenine, guanine, and cytosine). Each polynucleotide strand has a backbone of alternating sugar and phosphate linkages, with the nucleotides projecting inward from the sugar residues. Complementarity is due to the fact that, because of stereochemical constraints, the nucleotides of the two strands are joined by hydrogen bonds in such a manner that thymine (T) always pairs with adenine (A), and guanine (G) always pairs with cytocine (C). The paired nucleotides— A–T, T–A, G–C, C–G—can occur in any sequence along the length of the double helix; these constitute the basic elements of the so-called genetic alphabet. To give some idea of the number of nucleotides in a given individual, each somatic cell in a human being contains about 2.5 billion nucleotide pairs in its nucleus, with these divided between the forty-six chromo-

FIGURE 15   *The DNA double helix, represented in three different ways:
a) general picture of the double
helix, with the phosphate-sugar
combination making up the outside spirals and the base pairs the
cross bars; b) a more detailed
representation showing sugars
(S), phosphates (P), hydrogens
(H) which bond the bases in pairs
of adenine (A) and thymine (T) or
guanine (G) and cytosine (C);
and c) a more detailed representation to show how the space is
filled with atoms (actually the
space would be largely obliter-
ated by the closely packed atoms)
(Swanson 1973).*

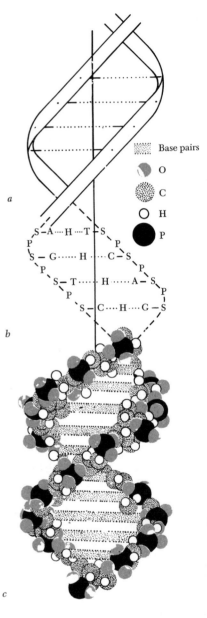

Base pairs

O

C

H

P

S—A····H····T—S
P   P
S — G······H····C—S
P   P
S—T······H····A—S
P   P
S—C····H····G—S

a

b

c

somes. The quality of complementarity gives stability to these huge molecules and determines their helical architecture as well, thus making possible their exact replication at each cell division.

However, a nucleotide or a nucleotide pair cannot be considered a source of information in the same manner that a letter in our English alphabet is a source of information; they are not equivalent units. It has been demonstrated that the individual nucleotides in a molecule of DNA are informationally inadequate because, in a biological sense, they cannot stand alone to be translated into retrievable and useful units for subsequent expression. The informational nature of a biogene comes, therefore, from the number and sequence of its nucleotides, together with whatever ancillary nucleotides are needed to make the information extractable. Each biogene is unique in its nucleotide number and sequence and represents, in a latent state, an emergent quality not previously deductible from its parts, in the same way that the quality of water is not deducible from knowledge of the individual qualities of oxygen and hydrogen.

FIGURE 16   *A schematic and flattened version of the double helix of DNA, showing the arrangement of the several molecules to form a macromolecular structure, with the two complementary spirals held together with hydrogen bonds. This arrangement twists in such a manner that there is a complete spiral for each ten nucleotide pairs (Swanson 1973).*

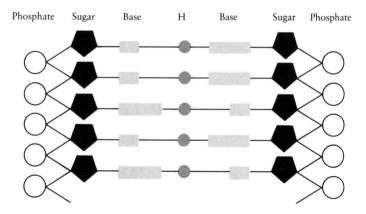

Phosphate   Sugar   Base   H   Base   Sugar   Phosphate

As scientists have become more and more adept at dissecting and analyzing the DNA of a species, it becomes obvious that not all blocks of DNA are potential sources of encoded information even though some segments of DNA may be, and often are, of greater molecular length than the typical biogene. The present view, therefore, is that the informational content is a regional and special, but not a general, character of DNA; this concept may be due to our limited knowledge of the potentiality and action of DNA, and there may be functions more subtly carried out than our present techniques permit us to detect.

The universality of inherited information

All cellular organisms of which we are aware have in common a DNA-based system of inherited information, with meaning built into the system by sequences of nucleotides, read three at a time at the moment of translation. This reading frame constitutes the so-called triplet code by which the information contained in DNA is deciphered. As intimated earlier, the precise and accurate transfer of this information from cell to cell, or, in sexual systems, from one generation to the next, depends on the fact that the two polynucleotide strands in the double helix are complementary to each other. Each strand, during replication, can be separated from its pairing partner, and, as separation occurs, the cellular machinery causes each complementary strand to reform the double helix. Thus two identical double helices are formed from its single predecessor, a process carried out with an extraordinarily small margin of error.

The release of information from this DNA-stored source rests upon the "readability" of the nucleotide sequence by appropriate cellular mechanisms which, on cue, begin to transform potential information into actuality. The expression of this information is first realized in the form of specific molecules of ribose nucleic acids (RNAs), some of which are subsequently translated into proteins. It is the proteins that confer biological uniqueness on every individual, either by contributing to the dynamic architecture of the cell, or by acting as enzymes (the

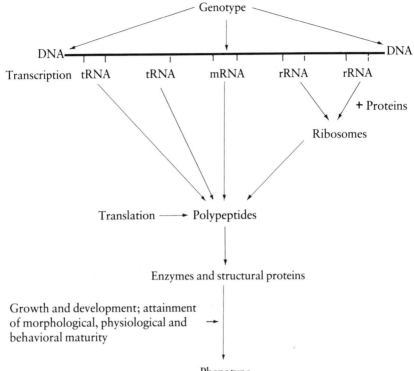

FIGURE 17   *Diagrammatic representation of the steps by which information en-coded in DNA is transcribed into the several forms of RNAs, trans-lated into various kinds of proteins, and matured and molded into spe-cific traits by the processes of growth and development (see fig. 21 for details of molecular change).*

organic catalysts that govern the kind and rate of chemical re-actions that take place at the cellular level). Because the several kinds of RNA which are required for the release of information are direct transcriptions of a complementary nature from DNA, the DNA of an organism is not only the source of coded infor-mation needed for the realization of its biological potential, it is also the source of the mechanisms for the release and regula-tion of that information as well.

We do not yet know how many eons it took for natural selection to bring this system of coded information and its orderly release to its present state of perfection. Certainly the system is far too complex and involves too many interacting biogenes to have arisen suddenly; a step-by-step process must have been involved, each step contributing its share to the size, stability, and workability of the information pool. It seems quite probable that the initial steps occurred very early in the history of life —the universality of DNA-based sources of inherited information suggests, but does not prove, this idea—with an assemblage of carbon-based molecules moving in the direction of stable configurations, acquiring the capacity of self-replication, and perfecting the means of extracting, for its own use, matter and energy from the immediate aqueous environment. The temporal relations of these events to the evolution of life in a cellular form remain uncertain. One can imagine that this period of information consolidation was a time of much random trial and error, with the margin of replication error decreasing as the means of capture and the flow of matter and energy became more and more systematized through the influence of natural selection; that is, any open-ended system such as a living organism, at whatever stage of development it is in, will become progressively more organized as energy flows into it, is converted to a particular use, and is then passed on to the environment at a lower energy level (fig. 6, Morowitz 1968). This increasing degree of orderly energy transfer and organization is not peculiar to living systems but, as Morowitz states, also holds true for "the environmental matrix in which biological systems can rise and flourish." It is brought into being out of the disorder of random building up and breaking down of organic substances, and it would be this process that would lead eventually to the emergent quality of life as we know it.

Without penetrating further into the realm of energy relationships and evolutionary strategies, it can nevertheless be stated that the increasing order (or decreasing entropy) of a system means an increase in the information of that system as well (Morowitz 1968). Molecules of whatever size have a greater degree of order and a larger content of information than do the atoms of which they are made. An emergent stability would, therefore, acquire a high selective value, and a trend would become established that would lead toward increasing the organization and, perhaps, the diversity and content of that information. To perpetuate, increase, and transfer that information is another matter and is dependent upon the acquisition of some kind of replicative device. If systems other than that with which we are familiar also arose, natural selection would be likely to have allowed but one to gain ascendance and to have hindered or eliminated the survival of others. As suggested earlier, this would account for the chemical uniformity of all cellular organisms at the same time that increasing complexity began to impose constraints on the possible direction and magnitude of future evolutionary change. That is, the more complex the system, and the more intricate the interactions of its parts, the more unlikely would it be that a perturbation in the system would have a significant effect other than one of a deleterious nature. Diversity would arise, however, and hence the possibilities of continued evolution, as the number of informational units increased. Environmental insults and replicative errors would add to the reservoir of diversity, but the incorporation of heritable innovations would be less tolerated, and the appearance of new qualities lessened, as complexity increased and stability resulted from the regulation and integration of grouped units. Evolution, to be sure, can only act on what is at hand. It moves in the direction of increased complexity because integrated complexity can deal more successfully with complex environments, but each added level of complexity introduces further constraints into the system. The testing of minor variations might well take place, but the striking out into new directions would be far less likely. If the history of early life may be likened to the tuning up of a symphony orchestra, the subsequent stages may be likened more to the playing of a fugue than to the continued introduction of new themes. Genuine evolutionary novelties are rare (Stebbins 1969).

The coded information of a fertilized egg destined to grow by epigenetic processes and rules into an individual of a recognizable species is parceled out among a number of biogenes, which themselves are grouped into the several chromosomes characteristic of that species. This information, however, is only of potential use until it is released from each biogene under appropriate circumstances of time and place by a series of enabling devices. These are the enzymatically mediated processes of *transcription* and *translation,* two critical intermediate steps along the pathway to phenotypic expression. To continue our musical metaphor, the programmed release of information is a performance of exquisite exactness, with all instruments coming in on cue, but, as indicated in the first chapter, what is at stake here is the "totality of an idea," that is, the genotype, expressed phenotypically as growth and development take place. It is only through such invariance that offspring resemble their parents and that species have a recognized existence beyond the life span of any single generation.

The nature of biogenes

Biogenes are of two general kinds: structural and regulatory. The structural variety are those that code for the great diversity of proteins found in the body of any individual plant, animal, or bacterium. Some biogenes function in every cell of a multicellular body, for example, those involved in energy transfer systems, or those coding for the enzymes of transcription or translation. Others function only in differentiated cells or under special circumstances; examples of these would be the ones coding for insulin in the beta cells of the pancreas or those that are responsible for the production and release of a particular immunoglobin when the body is subjected to the insult of a foreign protein. To appreciate the degree of precision with which the information coded in the biogenes of an individual can be realized in an expressed state, one need only recall the striking similarities of appearance and behavior of identical twins. In contrast to fraternal or dizygotic twins, they have their origin in a single fertilized egg and hence possess identical genetic constitutions. Passing through all the changes accompanying epi-

genetic processes of growth and development, including many
critical embryonic stages, they nevertheless retain shared physical and behavioral similarities despite being composed of bil-
lions of cells.

So deterministic a statement, however, may well be in need
of considerable qualification. Very little is known about how
embryonic processes are timed during development, and even
less is known about the inheritance of form. It has come as a
great surprise to realize that the percentage of DNA in a genome
making up the structural genes of higher organisms is very low,
probably no more than 1 or 2 percent of the total. An uncertain
amount consists of regulatory genes which are presumed to
govern the actions of their structural counterparts, with the remainder of the DNA having undetermined functions or, which
is perhaps more difficult to understand, none at all. A good deal
is known about the structure and action of the regulatory genes
in microorganisms and the structural genes of many higher species, but until the role of all the DNA in a genome is understood,
our knowledge of inheritance at all stages of the life cycle will
be incomplete. It might be assumed, for example, that there
should be a close relation between the number of structural and
regulatory biogenes and the complexity of an organisms, but
two difficulties present themselves: it is most difficult to define
"complexity" in an objective or quantitative manner, and the
amount of DNA per nucleus does not bear any clear-cut relation
to evolutionary advancement in either the plant or animal
kingdom.

Returning to a consideration of identical twins, but bearing
in mind the uncertainties above, it would appear that the genotype of an individual, composed of an organized and integrated
collection of structural and regulatory biogenes, possesses the
requisite stability to determine the persistence of the genotype
through many cell divisions, as well as the responsiveness to as-
yet-to-be-determined signals and constraints to govern the
timed release of information throughout the course of growth
and development. At the same time it is equally apparent that
the genome is not so intolerant of change that it cannot harbor

the mutations that provide the diversity upon which evolution acts.

Biogenetic constancy

Genotypic stability is expressed at three levels of organization, but with a different principle involved at each level. At the molecular level the principle of complementarity of paired nucleotides and the process of semiconservative replication enable DNA to exist as a stable double helix instead of as a more vulnerable single polynucleotide strand, while permitting each of the two polynucleotide strands to reconstitute itself again as a double helix. The process functions with a high degree of fidelity and is made even more exact by the presence in virtually all species of one or more error-correcting, or repair, mechanisms. Thus, incorrect nucleotides may be inserted into the growing polynucleotide strand as replication proceeds, but the repair enzymes have the capacity to "sense" these mistakes, to remove them, and then to allow replication to proceed again without error. Even so, some copy-errors pass through the detecting screen; these are mutations at the molecular level. Since the replicating enymes are "error blind," the mutations are as faithfully replicated as their unmutated predecessors were, but they are of no evolutionary or physiological consequence if they exist solely at the level of DNA. It is only when the biogene is activated that difficulties may appear. The structural or regulatory biogene itself may be inactivated by the insertion of an incorrect nucleotide at its time of formation (a gain or loss of a nucleotide can produce effects of comparable magnitude), the protein formed by the altered structural biogene may be nonfunctional or impaired by having its shape distorted, or the mutation may be neutral, leaving the protein unaltered in conformation or an amino acid changed in a noncritical portion of the molecule. These, however, are among the diversities upon which natural selection acts.

At a higher and chromosomal level of informational organization, the process of replication, coupled with the mechanisms of nuclear and cell division, makes it possible that each cell of the body or each individual in unicellular populations has the same inherited information as every other cell or individual. Accidents of cell division do occur, and somatic mutations or cell differentiation may occur to distinguish one cell from another, but it is only when the vast majority of cells have the same genetic constitution that selective action can occur during epigenetic development, making it possible for cells in a multicellular body to undergo differentiation at the same time that the conservation of the species is maintained.

At a still higher level of organization and complexity, the processes of gamete formation and sexual reproduction guarantee the transmission of coded information from one generation to the next, but with far more variance than those at the molecular or cellular levels. Sexual reproduction introduces biparentalism into the transmission picture, and, because the gametes differ genetically among themselves as a result of mei-

FIGURE 18

Replication of the DNA double helix. As the double helix separates into its two polynucleotide strands, two complementary strands are formed by the metabolic machinery of the cell. When the process is complete, the two strands are identical to each other, and to the original double helix (Swanson 1973).

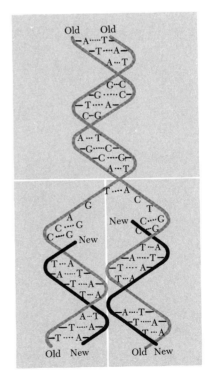

otic recombination and segregation, the offspring will be correspondingly different one from the other. The informational level of structures and performances, however, will maintain species identity, and the invariance at lower levels is in no way compromised at higher levels of organization. These are the conservative aspects of evolution.

The drive to replicate—DNA to more DNA, chromosomes to more chromosomes, cells to more cells, individuals to more individuals—is an attribute of life at several levels, the basis of self-preservation and of self-perpetuation. As Dawkins (1976) argues, the replicators are survival machines, and that is what

FIGURE 19   *Forms of reproduction taking place within most higher forms of life, including the human species. The degree of precision is lessened, and with increasingly more variable results, as one goes from the molecular, to the cellular, to the individual forms of reproduction. Evolution, however, could not take place if the degree of precision were absolute.*

Form of reproduction	Process	Degree of precision
DNA → DNA	Replication	Very low copy-error, aided by repair mechanisms. Errors by gain or loss of nucleotides, or their incorrect insertion.
Cell → Cell	Cell division or mitosis	Highly accurate, although gains or losses of chromosomes occur, but are not serious in a somatic cell.
Generation → Generation	Gamete formation (meiosis), and fertilization	Meiosis involves recombination of genes and chromosomes, and fertilization is the random union of eggs and sperm. Source of diverse genotypes. Any human offspring having more or less than the normal number of chromosomes is subnormal.

evolution is all about. Ordinarily the drive is toward stability, toward a measure of homeostasis, if you will, but when environmental changes of varying severity occur, the shifts in the patterns of survival are asserted. It has been suggested that significant environmental changes during geological periods have resulted in outbursts of new species and genera or the wiping out of great groups of organisms. On a more restricted and local level, Lewis (1973), for example, has shown that drastic ecological change such as drought can reduce populations of the plant *Clarkia* to a few individuals, force inbreeding and homozygosity, and result in an outburst of speciation in marginal ecological areas. The effect of environmental pressures on a replicator can be demonstrated even more dramatically in a test tube (Mills et al. 1973). Thus, a replicating molecule, in this instance a molecule of RNA rather than DNA, was provided with the requisite substrate and enzymes but was subject to intense selective pressure which favored rapid replication. After a relatively few rounds of replication, the molecules had lost all nucleotide pairs except those required for replication and in the process had reduced themselves to only 12 percent of their initial length. Other highly selective regimens favor the creation of similar, but different, molecules, indicating that the replicator can maintain itself, albeit in altered form, while responding to external influences.

In cellular systems, and at higher multicellular levels of organization, self-preservation cannot be dissociated from self-maintenance, and the latter is possible only with the continued release of information necessary to sustain it. Thus, a flow of information from an encoded to an expressed state—from DNA to proteins—is mandatory if the matter and energy required by a system is to be acquired; this is carried out through the processes of transcription and translation. To be sure, an amoeba or a red blood cell can be deprived of its nucleus, the site of its biogenes, without causing an immediate cessation of vital processes, but both kinds of cells will eventually run down and die because of a lack of self-maintenance ability, and neither, of course, will be able to perpetuate itself through cell division.

Information retrieval

The release of encoded information from any kind of storage system—library, computer, or genome—requires the active use of a retrieval system or an enabling device. When released from the DNA of the genome, the initial step is that of transcription, a molecular process similar to replication in that it is based on the complementarity of nucleotides, but differing in that it leads to the formation of several kinds of single-stranded RNAs instead of more DNA in double helical form. Further, and in contrast to replication, transcription involves, at any given time, only selected parts of the genome rather than all of it. A number of biogenes are involved: one class is transcribed into a "message" that, in the form of messenger RNA (mRNA), leaves the site of its formation in the genome and travels to a subsequent site where it will be "read" by appropriate cellular mechanisms; another class of biogenes is transcribed to produce ribosomal RNA (rRNA) that, together with a group of special proteins, will form the ribosomes, the cytoplasmic site of attachment for the mRNA; and still another class of biogenes will be transcribed to form the many kinds of transfer RNAs

FIGURE 20

The formation of a message in the form of messenger RNA during the process of transcription. The double helix of DNA "opens" up, and only one of the two polynucleotide strands is to be decoded and sent out into the cytoplasm as a message. The mRNA (bottom strand) is complementary to the strand of DNA which is being "read" by an enzyme, transcriptase, with the exception that thymine is replaced in RNA by a comparable nucleotide, uracil (U). When fully transcribed, the RNA is released.

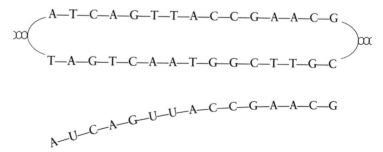

(tRNAs) needed to decode or "read" the message in the mRNAs and bring it to an expressed state in the form of a protein. The decoding process is known as translation since the message encoded in a nucleic acid form is to be realized and expressed as a protein, a quite different kind of molecule. The role of the tRNAs is, once again, dependent upon the principle of complementarity; each tRNA, of which there may be as many as sixty-one, contains an anticode for interacting with the message. As it interacts, it brings into position an amino acid that is specifically related to the anticode, which will be built in to a polypeptide which the message defines. Because there are only four kinds of nucleotides in a single-stranded mRNA—A, U (uracil, which replaces thymine in all RNAs), G, and C—which govern the exact placing of the twenty essential amino acids that are found in proteins, the coded message and the complementary anticodes of the translating tRNAs are based on a triplet system. Thus, three adjacent nucleotides in the mRNA, and three complementary nucleotides in the anticode of tRNA, are required to specify one amino acid in a polypeptide. The four nucleotides, taken three at a time ($4 \times 4 \times 4$), constitute a total of sixty-four triplet codes, more than enough to take care of twenty amino acids, even though three of the triplets act as terminating signals for the message, while the remaining triplets show varying degrees of redundancy. For example, the amino acid serine is specified by six different triplet codes, threonine by four, phenylalanine by two, and methionine by only one. A message is translated, therefore, in blocks of three nucleotides at a time and in a given direction. Since it also has specified initiation and termination points, a message in an mRNA shows a striking analogy to a sentence in a human language.

Interestingly enough, transcription does not always produce a finished message in the form of mRNA ready to be translated. Rather, it usually leads to the formation of a much longer heterogeneous RNA (hnRNA) which undergoes a transformation before it is ready to be decoded. The message must be equipped with beginning and terminal signals, complexed with a unique set of nuclear proteins, and, in some instances, brought to a

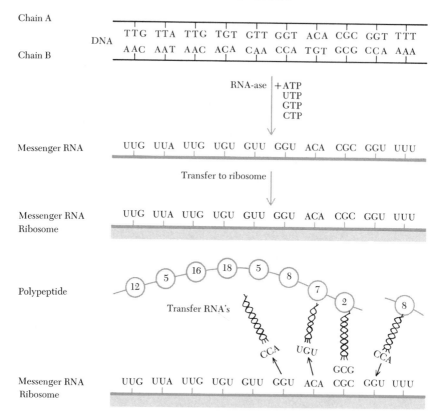

Chain A

DNA

Chain B

TTG TTA TTG TGT GTT GGT ACA CGC GGT TTT
AAC AAT AAC ACA CAA CCA TGT GCG CCA AAA

RNA-ase +ATP
UTP
GTP
CTP

Messenger RNA

UUG UUA UUG UGU GUU GGU ACA CGC GGU UUU

Transfer to ribosome

Messenger RNA
Ribosome

UUG UUA UUG UGU GUU GGU ACA CGC GGU UUU

Polypeptide

Transfer RNA's

Messenger RNA
Ribosome

UUG UUA UUG UGU GUU GGU ACA CGC GGU UUU

FIGURE 21

The sequence of events whereby the information encoded in the DNA molecule is transcribed into a particular message (messenger RNA, or mRNA) and then, by translation, into the form of a particular protein. It is assumed here that it is the B chain of the DNA which is being transcribed. The mRNA contains the information to be decoded. The mRNA is first moved from the nucleus of the cell to the cytoplasm, where it becomes associated with a number of small bodies, or ribosomes, made up of rRNA and proteins. The reading of the message in the mRNA is carried out by a series of transfer RNAs, or tRNAs, each of which possesses a particular anticode. The reading is done in blocks of three nucleotides, with the tRNAs pairing with the message in a complementary manner. Each tRNA carries with it a particular amino acid, and as the message is being read, these amino acids become attached to adjacent ones to establish the growing protein or polypeptide. Once the amino acid has become attached, the tRNA moves away and is free to pick up another amino acid for future use (modified from Swanson and Webster 1977).

"readable" state by the excision of intervening blocks of non-translatable nucleotides, followed by the union of the remaining RNA to make a completed message (e.g., Pederson 1981). It must be evident that such a complicated, beautifully integrated patterning of processing, which is comparable to the similarly intricate DNA $\longrightarrow$ RNA $\longrightarrow$ polypeptide sequence of events, could not have arisen in evolutionary history except through a sequence of successive and selected-for changes in the management of the genome itself.

It is of further interest to point out that, although the entire process of polypeptide formation as the first phenotypic expression of a biogene is a closely regulated system, there appears to be no error-correcting mechanism at the level of transcription or translation comparable to that associated with replication. One can hazard a guess that such mechanisms, which exact their own cost in materials and energy, are not really needed. Any given message in the form of mRNA is of a temporary character. It is capable of being translated but for only a few times, and if the mRNA message happens to be a faulty one and is translated into a faulty polypeptide, no great cellular harm is done. Even if it is, the damage is more than likely to be temporary and local. Further, the unimpaired biogene can be transcribed in repeated fashion to produce correct messages. In evolutionary terms, therefore, no significant selective pressure arose to guarantee a high level of accuracy of transcription and translation, and as a consequence no repair mechanisms evolved to screen out errors.

The expression of a genetic message as well as its role in the sequential events of growth and development must be closely regulated phenomena, temporally and spatially, although we do not yet understand all of the nuances involved. Expression may be as close to the transcriptional event as the involvement of the rRNAs in the formation of ribosomes or the insertion of a newly formed polypeptide into the membrane of an active cell; as deferred in ontogeny as the attainment of sexual maturity or the graying of hair; as dependent for full expression as the alpha protein of hemoglobin which must unite with the beta protein and a heme group before its usefulness in the blood stream can be realized; as presently meaningless to the survival of a human being as the ability to curl one's tongue or to wiggle one's ears; or as central to continued existence as the biosynthesis of chlorophyll is to a green plant. Any genome is both an echo of past history as well as an expression of present needs.

The collective biogenes of any organism constitute, therefore, a storehouse of inherited information, encoded in extractable form and pertinent to its participation in an evolving world. As Blakemore (1977) has expressed it, the double helix of DNA is both a genetic memory and a code, "a receipt for replicating the structure of that organism." For some species these inherited and transmitted genes represent their entire dictionary of information; they are equipped to acquire materials and energy from the environment and to convert these for their own use but are ill-equipped to acquire additional information through experience. Other species can expand their source of information through a process of learning, and to that extent they possess both an inherited and an acquired pool of knowledge (Bonner 1980). Their flexibility in adapting to varied circumstances is in direct proportion to their learning capability. The human species, of course, is unique in this respect, but before inquiring into how and to what degree inherited or acquired diversity provides the variation required for evolutionary change and before losing the thread of thought expressed in the preceding pages, it will be well to examine the informational base of cultural evolution and to make such cross-level comparisons with organic evolution as are possible or feasible.

Homeostasis: maintaining a steady state

Geertz (1966) has described culture as a phenomenon based on "sets of control mechanisms"; the parallel with the homeostatic mechanisms of an organic nature is obvious, although any organism capable of learning from progressively encountered experiences is more than a set of such mechanisms. As discussed earlier, complexity of structure and behavior has increased, and perceived horizons have expanded, as vertebrate evolution has taken place, and the neural circuitry required for the integrated expression of this complexity has been similarly increased in extent and intricacy. It is for this reason, if for no other, that genuine innovation in evolution is rare; physical and physiological integration is based on many inherited and coordinated parts, and evolution is more likely than not to consist of variation on a theme. The integrated neural circuitry, which is genetically determined, acts as a powerful constraint to the rate of change since abrupt change would very likely overburden and disrupt the circuitry (Bateson 1963).

In order that the conscious management of this growing complexity not overwhelm a species, control of the routine but vital facets of existence, notably those of a physiological nature, has been taken over by homeostatic mechanisms which respond automatically to specific internal and external signals. In a vertebrate species the principal organic result of homeostasis is the controlled functioning of the "fluid matrix" of the body, the "rapidly flowing blood and the more slowly moving lymph" (Cannon 1939). Through transportation and distribution as well as by its own constancy of volume and composition, the fluid matrix serves all parts of the body, enabling those parts to meet their needs of food, water, oxygen, energy, appropriate temperature, and the removal of wastes while they perform their essential and special tasks. Organizational stability is achieved, as is a significant measure of economy, in that each organ, indeed each cell, need not be supplied nor concerned with its own governing systems. It is difficult to imagine, for example, how the central nervous system, the principal source of cultural innovation and direction, could function properly if its temperature were fluctuating constantly or if its food and energy requirements were met in a haphazard fashion (Crawshaw et al. 1981).

Analogous approaches to homeostatic stability and economy may be observed at the level of society as well. As social complexity increases, so too does the need for the control of those functions essential to identity, stability, and survival.

Thus, increasing social complexity places a greater emphasis on learned behavior, and, as a result, there is a gradual shift in the control of behavior from the biogenotype to the environment. That is, the environment—physical, biological, psychological, and social—takes on an increasingly significant role as the source of instruction for the individual, aiding in the "fixation of experience" of a cultured animal (Gerard 1961). The constancy of a culture indicates that its homeostatic mechanisms are functioning or are capable of being called into immediate action should the circumstances dictate. Under these conditions, the social environment as the source of instruction can be said to be exerting its controlling functions. To the extent that an environmental pressure is unrelenting in its effects, a response to that pressure will be gradually built into the biogenotype by the incorporation and fixation of randomly occurring but appropriate mutations; but if environmental changes take place so rapidly that the biogenotype is unable to accommodate to them, then selection will favor either increased plasticity in the phenotype of individuals or increased flexibility of the learning pattern. The function of cultural homeostasis is to reduce the effects of fluctuating environmental and social changes to tolerable levels. As Cannon (1939) sees it from the point of view of a physiologist, the main service of cultural organization would be to support bodily homeostasis, helping thereby to liberate a portion of the central nervous system from the management of the routine tasks of existence and to free it "for adventure and achievement." Alfred North Whitehead put it somewhat differently: "Civilization advances by extending the number of important operations which we can perform without thinking about them." Such remarks are no more than special instances of a more general evolutionary phenomenon, that is, that selection at all levels favors the survival of that which is stable (Ashby 1960; Slobodkin 1964; Dawkins 1976). In the human realm our human uniqueness is achieved, somewhat paradoxically, by an increase in behavioral or somatic flexibility (Bateson 1963), but this is possible only because of the existence of other stabilizing influences.

Geertz (1966) has put these thoughts into a more direct cultural frame of reference: "undirected by cultural patterns, man's behavior would be virtually ungovernable, a chaos of pointless acts and exploding emotions, his experience virtually shapeless." Evolution could lead to little more than survival in the presence of high levels of social chaos. But however important control mechanisms are to a culture, and homeostatic mechanisms to a species, they are but the phenotypic reflections of more fundamental informational bases. To define a species in terms of its homeostatic mechanisms is hardly sufficient because every facet of bodily homeostasis, as well as many other features of the phenotype, is determined by one or more, and probably many, biogenes and brought into functional expression by the enabling devices of transcription, translation, and differential growth and development. It is proposed here that an equivalent situation exists at the cultural level and that Geertz's control mechanisms, as well as other aspects of cultural phenotypes, are determined by the integrated actions of many *sociogenes,* the cultural counterpart of the biogenes that determine the phenotype of each species and individual.

The sociogene

A *sociogene* is defined here as a mental concept, a structured image, arising from one or more acts of experience, molded into shape and integrated with other sociogenes by the action of the central nervous system and from which information is extractable, expressible, and transmissible within the context of a social milieu. Unlike biogenes, sociogenes do not have a detectable molecular structure; they are mental abstractions and they are, therefore, that much more difficult to define and characterize. Adding to the difficulties of identification is the relative ease with which a sociogene can lose its dimensional clarity as it becomes submerged in the general sociogenotype of a culture. Its continued presence, however, is made evident when a mutant form of a sociogene arises, necessitating its removal from the genotypic matrix so that comparisons and appraisals can be made. But these difficulties make them no less real than biogenes. If this loose definition of a sociogene gives one pause, it need be but pointed out that for the first fifty years of its recognized existence the biogene was also an abstraction (Stadler 1954).

The concept of a sociogene as the evolving unit of cultural evolution in no way invalidates or diminishes the significance of material artifacts or of language as aspects of culture. They obviously have an evolutionary role, but it is a derivative and not a basic one. Rather, the attempt being made here is to focus on that which seems to be the informational basis, the DNA,

FIGURE 22   *The origin of a sociogene. The biological features are determined by biogenes, but the acuity of discrimination at the sensory level can be modified by experience, and there is evidence that the intricacies of neuronal connections in the central nervous system depend to a degree on environmental diversity or monotony during formative stages.*

Level of Action

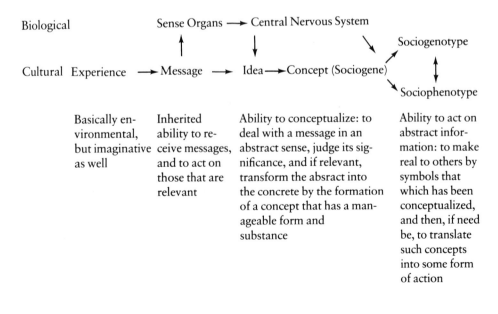

Biological		Sense Organs ⟶ Central Nervous System		Sociogenotype
Cultural Experience ⟶	Message ⟶	Idea ⟶ Concept (Sociogene)		Sociophenotype
Basically environmental, but imaginative as well	Inherited ability to receive messages, and to act on those that are relevant	Ability to conceptualize: to deal with a message in an abstract sense, judge its significance, and if relevant, transform the absract into the concrete by the formation of a concept that has a manageable form and substance		Ability to act on abstract information: to make real to others by symbols that which has been conceptualized, and then, if need be, to translate such concepts into some form of action

if you will, of cultural evolution, and then to compare it with the biogene itself. The sociogene, as defined here, meets this criterion.

Just as cultural evolution is but a variation of organic evolution, so indeed are sociogenes derivative of the collective biogenes of a species but only in an indirect sense. That is, they are products of a nervous system that is genetically determined, but the relation to biogenes is not on a one-to-one basis, and they exist in an entirely different form. The forerunners of some cultural elements are evident in other vertebrate (particularly primate) groups, but the existence of sociogenes presupposes the prior existence of a high level of sensory and neural complexity, a retentive memory, an ability to conceptualize, a growing sense of self-awareness and of separateness from the environment, and a high level of behavioral flexibility. The origin and expression of sociogenes are, therefore, largely within the human species. The name of the game, however, is still evolution, and the goal, if such it can be called, remains the survival of the stable in the face of change. The rules of the evolutionary game are also the same, even if the basis of information, the environment, and the selective mechanisms are different. The collective expression of the sociogenes, through the medium of their own enabling device(s), represents a genuine innovation in evolutionary history, the emergence of a new quality that we call culture and with it the emergence of man. We need to be cautious, however, in attributing innovativeness to the human species alone (Bonner 1980), for the novelty of qualitative change may be evident only at the end of a long and slow process of quantitative transformation.

The genesis of a sociogene, however well or poorly it may be delineated initially, is in the mind of a single individual exposed to the impact of a prodding experience. As Boulding (1956) has emphasized, the significance as well as the meaning of an experiential message lies in the changes it induces in the previously held mental image. The possible retention of a sociogene, and its incorporation into the sociogene pool of a culture, can occur only if it is transformed from a vague image into a concept having sufficient structure and content to be taken from a private into a public form. A mental image is a potential sociogene only if it can be shared by others with mutual understanding and acceptance; it dies with the individual, a wasted opportunity, if it does not become public. Sociogenes, therefore, share a common aspect with biogenes: some make it, others do not; yet all, nonetheless, are genes of a sort. The resultant sociophenotype will include the control mechanism of Geertz (1966), as well as much else of human expression, and presumably will attain its manifestations through some form of cultural development, possibly the epigenetic pathways of Lumsden and Wilson (1981).

Each human individual, while capable of originating sociogenes and thus enriching his own conceptual storehouse, develops his basic sociogenotype by learning and gains his experiences within the "multiparental" context of a social group rather than through biparental sexual inheritance. It is in the act of going public that a sociogene acquires its cultural potency and becomes a part of the "communal intellect—the Collective Mind of man" (Blakemore 1977). It is a piece of shared information that establishes a bond between individuals, a form of organization that promotes social coherence, and at the same time, through the processes of epigenesis, helps to spare other individuals "an immense amount of individualized learning" (Murdock 1960). The sociogenotype, however, cannot be divorced from the biogenotype. Its dependence is a direct one since the acquisition of a sociogenotype in a fully functional social state is made possible only if the recipient possesses the appropriate neural equipment and mental capability.

Sociogenes: a comparative appraisal

The term *sociogene* needs further justification. It was first used in a somewhat casual manner (Swanson 1973), but it has been retained in preference to other similar terms in order to keep its meaning confined within a social context, as well as to indicate its informational equivalence with a biogene. The term *cul-*

turgen of Lumsden and Wilson (1981) is defined as a basic unit of culture and collectively as "a relatively homogeneous set of artifacts, behaviors and mentifacts (mental constructs having little or no direct correspondence to reality) that either shares without exception one or more attribute states selected for their functional importance or at least shares a consistently recurrent range of such attribute sets within a given polythetic set." Despite extensive documentation relative to their general thesis, Lumsden and Wilson's definition is all-encompassing, a catchall addressed to culture as a whole rather than to a basic evolving unit. Their *mentifact* has a correspondence to the *sociogene* as used here, but their artifacts and many forms of behavior, however reflexive or involuntary the latter might become through acceptance and constant use, are derivative phenomena, based on mental constructs previously formulated and learned largely by rote or example. The term is rejected on two other bases as well. The protean nature of the definition allows it to be loosely used and hence reduces its effectiveness, and for me (perhaps because I am a botanist) it shares too close a similarity with the term *cultigen,* a word commonly used by ethnobotanists to designate a plant of apparent specific rank but known only in cultivation and with no recognized native affiliations.

Huxley (1958) first employed the term *mentifact* to embrace the mental images, assumptions, ideas, values, traditions, and intentions of a culture, but he also used *sociofacts* to cover rituals and *artifacts* for such things as stone implements. Whether Huxley considered them to be of parallel and equal importance is not clear, but in the view offered here the latter two definitions (and some aspects of the first) would be the products of sociogenes and hence of derivative origin. Blum (1963) and Campbell (1966) define their units of cultural inheritance more nearly as the sociogene is defined here. Blum, for example, coined the term *mnemotype* (from the Greek *mnemonikos,* to remember) as the cultural equivalent of the biogenotype, defining it as "the personal collection of memory images in a single brain." The probable implication to be drawn would be that a *mneme* is the equivalent of the sociogene. Campbell has stated that "ritual is, as it were, the DNA of society," meaning thereby "the encoded informational basis of culture; it is the memory core of human social achievement." Campbell's *ritual* is thus to be identified more closely with the sociogene than it is with Huxley's *sociofact,* but ritual is generally defined as ceremonial procedures rather than as their informational base. More recently, Dawkins (1976) has added still another term with a somewhat different meaning. In the context of his "selfish gene" hypothesis in which the organism is subservient to the gene as the replicator, he has sought a term that would represent the replicator of cultural evolution. The term *meme,* an abbreviation of *mimene* (from the Greek *mimēsis,* imitation) was coined to serve as "a unit of cultural transmission, or a unit of *imitation*" (his italics). As with Lumsden and Wilson's *culturgen,* Dawkins's term is another cultural catchall: in his words "memes are tunes, ideas, catch-phrases, clothes, fashions, ways of making pots or of building arches. Just as genes propagate themselves in the gene pool by leaping from body to body via sperms or eggs, so memes propagate themselves in the meme pool by leaping from brain to brain via a process which, in the broad sense, can be called imitation." If one can assume that Dawkins means that it is ideas or concepts that leap from "brain to brain," then the meme and the sociogene are not too far different from each other in meaning.

Clearly all of these terms and definitions share much in common in that they deal wholly or in part with the ability of man not just to perceive and to experience but also to develop images, to conceptualize, and to formulate abstract ideas with sufficient clarity so that they can be made public and shared with others. It is in this sense that the central nervous system takes on, as it were, a life of its own and can transcend its organic origins. Some of these sociogenes will be shared by everyone in a culture, thus establishing its basic form, including the control mechanisms of Geertz (1966). But sociogenes, like biogenes, are of bewildering diversity; they include all the mental concepts of man, however permanent or transitory, which flow through a social group, which are accepted, rejected, mulled over, modified, fought for, forgotten, or recalled, and which, because of their very diversity, are the ingredients of disorder out of which new patterns of order evolve. The sociogenes of any single individual are not a total reflection of the total gene pool of a culture any more than his biogenes are of the total gene pool of a species. However, each of us shares enough of certain kinds of genes to allow us to qualify not only as recognizable members of the human species but also as members of the culture in which we have our being. It would be the unshared genes, in different combinations, that would provide each of us with an individual uniqueness.

Experiences and images

Be they sociogenes, mnemes, or memes, they are evidence of the extraordinary ability of the human species to dissect the physical, biological, and social environments into tangible and unique units of things or events, to incorporate, manipulate, and integrate these units into mental and hence abstract concepts, to store them in a memory bank from which they can be retrieved, to share them with others by means of appropriate symbols or by imitation, and to use them, individually and socially, to give meaning and significance to human existence.

It is unlikely that the human species is unique in its possession of sociogenes. Any animal moving purposely through time and space cannot help acquiring a memory bank of experiential images that will affect and direct its future behavior. Depending on the species, these images will supplement instinctual responses to environmental signals and together will assist an individual in responding to varying circumstances and encountered challenges. The biological and social significance of any act of experience, therefore, is the role it plays in the modification of old, or the formation of new, sociogenes and the subsequent impact that newly arisen or modified sociogenes will have on the total sociogenotype. The human species, so limited in its repertoire of instinctual responses, is almost wholly dependent on the ability to acquire a sociogenotype and to express it ultimately as a sociophenotype. Whether this acquisition is a channeled one and follows the epigenetic rules of Lumsden and Wilson (1981) is yet to be established.

Images have their origin extrasomatically as environmentally generated signals. Even abstract ideas, however remote they may be from a tangible reality, have their origins from some previous, perhaps now forgotten, signals. Every object and every event in the environment emits an identifying signal, and all organisms are constantly being bombarded by signals of every sort, received through their sensory receptors. If all signals were of equal importance, and if an organism were unable to exercise selectivity of reception, the noise would be such as to flood the receiving, integrating, and motor circuits of the mind, and only chaos would be experienced. Survival, therefore, dictates that there be a way of ignoring meaningless messages, for allowing those that are relevant to filter through, and for perfecting a response to them. As learning has taken over from epigenetically programmed instincts as a means of directing behavior, a time lag has been built into the process of response, a lag during which the cortical portions of the brain come into play and an appraisal of the incoming signal is made. The importance of this time lag between receiving a signal and responding to it cannot be overemphasized, for it is that which permits the exercise of choice and the selecting of an option from among the possibilities presented. The acquisition of a background of meaningful information becomes a process of discriminatory selection and organization. Human evolution, consequently, has moved in the direction of enhancing behavioral flexibility. As Bateson (1963) has put it, the winning hand in a poker game may be various indeed, but the particular hand and the way it is played cannot be foreordained.

Each species, indeed each individual, lives in a world of its own, shared only partially with others of its own group. It defines its own reality as it grinds the lenses of its mind's eye. The quality of the mental lenses will determine which messages will penetrate to the level of consciousness, where an appraisal will lead to the retention of those that might modify, enrich, and, possibly, become inserted into the existing sociogenotype. New images, of course, can be generated by reordering the elements within the memory bank of the mind and without the immediate prompting of a message from an environmental object or event, and encountered acts of experience may be startlingly new and unfamiliar; but the reception, fate, and impact of each is determined or conditioned by the experience of the past, whether that past is acquired through sexual or learned inheritance. Events may be unprecedented, but responses to them are not.

Biogenes and sociogenes possess, therefore, a cross-level identity in the sense that they are collectively the basic sources of information of their respective evolving systems. We have seen that the diversities of the biological world became much more understandable through a knowledge of DNA and its role in inheritance and evolution; it is to be hoped that a similar understanding of the diversities of culture can be gained through our knowledge of the nature and role of sociogenes in cultural matters. Both sets of genes are also similar in that they are silent forms of encoded information until released from their unexpressed state by an enabling, or retrieving, device. For biogenes, as earlier discussed, there are two levels of release: at the molecular level through the processes of transcription and translation, processes in which the several kinds of RNAs are the enabling devices that bring the polypeptides into existence; and subsequently at a higher level of organization, where the epigenetic processes of growth, differentiation, and development bring the biological information to its ultimate expression of form and function.

Symbols and sociogenes

The sociogenes provide a third level of release of information for the ordering of behavior, this by means of symboling. Imitation, conscious or unconscious, provides a route to learning, but its importance varies with the species in question. The piercing of a milk bottle cap to get at the cream by the great tit of England and the washing of food by the Japanese monkeys are examples of acts initiated by one individual and then acquired by others through imitation. But when compared to vocal symboling in the human species and its significance for teaching and learning (Bonner 1980), imitation of actions is an inefficient form of information release and distribution.

It is vocal symboling, or language and syntax, that is the principal means of establishing, defining, and maintaining the human cultural world as we know it. It is the process of reification (that is, considering subjective phenomena as objective entities) that distinguishes human beings from the members of all other species. As von Foerster (1966) has said, language is the principal tool of a single species for transforming the natural world into a human world, the means of freeing "ideas from the general formlessness of the external world" and of putting ideas into a cage of form. Franz Kafka, in a passage whose source I can no longer identify, said that "A book should serve as the axe for the frozen sea within us." Symbols have the same function. They tend to shear the fuzziness from, and sharpen the outlines of, mental concepts and in the process reveal the structure, intricacy, and style of the human mind. Shared with others who accept symbols for their abstract worth, symbols also serve as bonding elements, integrating related concepts into a larger unity which then may gain visibility as a part of the phenotype of a culture.

Lenski and Lenski (1978) have contended that *"symbol systems are the functional equivalent of the genetic alphabet"* (their italics), but it is suggested here that such a definition confuses the process of expression with the substance of that which is being expressed. Symbols are enabling devices, the RNAs of culture, not its DNA.

Symbols, and most particularly those of a linguistic nature, are largely inventions of the human species, although they are not without antecedents. Collectively, they constitute a system for expressing our vision of reality, of the world around us, and, in the process, of investing that world with meaning. A symbol, in fact, is without meaning until it has been invested with a factual, ideological, or emotional content. The relation between the symbol and the sociogene, between a word and an image, is therefore wholly arbitrary, standing for or taking the place of real things or events in the real world of experience. Symbols are for reflective information as well as for the isolated bits and pieces of instruction and communication embedded in signals. When freed of any initial ambiguity and brought to the level of communal use by constant repetition, symbols tend to transcend the limits of time, place, and circumstances and to take on a kind of permanence of their own. Anything labeled is less likely to be forgotten. In contrast to the universality and invariance of the RNAs in the DNA $\longrightarrow$ RNA $\longrightarrow$ polypeptide sequence of organic events, symbols are far more diversified in character. Because they have their use at the end of a time lag that separates an environment signal from a possible response, they are far more plastic in the relation between the sociogene and its expression.

Language intensifies and liberates an act of experience and its resultant image by the simple process of lifting it out of the matrix of surrounding confusion and circumscribing it by giving it an identity and a form. It is, first of all, an integrating mechanism and only secondarily a means of communication (Jerison 1976). It is also, in a sense, an impoverishing act. The invention or use of a symbol is a selective act, and hence it limits interpretation; it is a means of turning "*the* world into *this* world" (Boulding 1956), which may be only one of many possible worlds. It is to these symbols, then, to these extractors of images, that the human species generally responds and out of which the world of shared knowledge is constructed. It is by way of symbols that the private image becomes sufficiently tangible to be appraised, reshaped, and possibly incorporated into the public sociogenotype. Viewed in this manner, human sociogenes and their symbolic representation express what is human about the human species, and cultural evolution can be redefined as the changing pool of sociogenes, their changed expression through symboling, and their transmission through time. Although the shift from a hominoid to a hominid state required many changes of structure and behavior, it was probably the successful merging of imaging and an abstract language that has resulted in the expression of so much of that which is peculiarly human about us. It was a Rubicon that took an unknown number of eons to cross, but once crossed it came to separate us irrevocably from our pongid predecessors (Isaac 1979). The chimpanzees, of course, effectively use symbols for communication, but a matter of degree is perceived as qualitative rather than quantitative when the gap is sufficiently widened. The human species, therefore, may be viewed as the avant-garde of the primate world, that segment of an assemblage of species that at sometime, somehow, and somewhere (most likely in East Africa) broke for themselves the linkage that has kept the remaining primate species in the prison of their animality.

As intimated, this leap forward must have created a distinct discontinuity within the protohuman group, a gap that contin-. ued to widen with time and to lead eventually to an irreversible separation of species. The tripling of the size of the brain over a span of several million years is the clearest morphological evidence that we have of this transformation, but it is unlikely that the increase in neural mass, a subject of much debate among those concerned with human origins, can be attributed solely to a greater aptitude for verbalization. There are no special speech centers in the brain, although about 20 percent of the brain is concerned with the control of the lips, tongue, and larynx. The institution of gathering as a way of life probably introduced many new ways for doing things around an established site of residence, and it may well have been the young of the group who, with their capacity for accepting change and playful inventiveness, most successfully experimented with symboling until the obvious usefulness of it all penetrated through the resistance of even the elders of the group. Frank (1966) suggests that the early symbolizers may be likened to the poets of an age, juggling symbol, object, and concept until their connected appropriateness made them inseparable. Change, of course, is that upon which evolution feeds, and as

98

Van Wyck Brooks (1956) once pointed out in another context, "the avant-garde is useful in perpetually changing the air that [one] breathes." The practice of inventing abstract symbols to deal with all facets of human life continues unabated.

The effectiveness of symbols presupposes certain conditions (Savage-Rumbaugh et al. 1978, 1980): that there exists a storehouse of experiential images and knowledge to which an invented symbol can be referred or from which meaning can be extracted and applied to the symbol; that the symbol, through frequent use, be reasonably familiar to others yet flexible enough in its application so that its meaning may be perceived by those whose perception of an event or of an object can vary from that of the symboler; that the giver and receiver of a symbol have sufficiently overlapping or shared experiences so that the intentional use of a symbol will convey meaning; and that the symbol can be decoded and, if necessary, acted upon by the recipient. Theoretically, symbols can convey, within appropriately receptive groups, an infinite amount of information, probably far more than any individual imaging system can supply. As the primate-on-the-way-to-becoming-human was provided with expanded vistas to be encompassed and learned to dissect the environment into finer and finer details and thus, without altering the environmental constituents, created within its mind's eye an environment of increasing complexity, the symboling system at the same time had to be adequate to the task of translating these nuances into communicable shared experiences and of fixing them for future use. It is not simply word play that has led the Eskimo to invent about forty verbal symbols to describe the character of snow.

Despite the enormous potential and versatility of symbols, they are essentially enabling devices, a means of freeing the content of sociogenes from their cortical site and making them a communal property. Just as a segment of DNA that does not participate in, or that has no regulatory effect on, the DNA $\longrightarrow$ RNA sequence of events is a form of "silent" DNA, so too does a sociogene remain mute within the memory bank of an individual if it cannot be or has not been symbolized.

The invention of culture

The invention of a complex human culture was not an inevitability. It was made possible by the inheritance of many integrated mammalian changes, accumulating over long eons of time. Despite intimations of sociogenes among virtually all the higher primates observed in both wild and laboratory situations, human culture as we have come to know it emerged in East Africa but not in the Americas or in Asia, where the potentiality also existed for, but was never realized by, other primate groups. In the latter areas, the primate lines evolved in other directions. But culture, probably the most complex and successful adaptive phenomenon to arise in the biological world, could have happened only in a species that for one reason or another had previously attained a high level of neural and social complexity. What triggered the beginnings of cultural evolution and the emergence of the genus Homo may never be fully understood, but there is little question that it is the sensory system and the brain that link a species to its environment, govern its adaptive responses, and are the source of its sociogenes (Gerard 1960). Increasing complexity of whatever sort is accompanied by an increased number of neurons and neuronal connections, and the reception of and response to experience is not simply to be measured quantitatively but qualitatively as well. It is, after all, quality and not quantity of response that matters at this stage of evolution, although the quantity of information that can be managed must have been substantially increased as the hominid brain underwent a significant enlargement during the Pleistocene and pre-Pleistocene years. The qualitative change that was important was a shift in learning patterns, a shift that led from a racial (biogenetic) to an individual (sociogenetic) learning base.

Imaging and the art of symboling must have come into being at quite different times during the course of evolution. The former is an inherited feature of any organism that has the capability of learning through its perception of its environment (Bonner 1980), while the latter became gradually transformed from the instinctual, stereotyped vocalization of less advanced species to the open-ended and flexible repertoire of color and tone of human speech. The two would also have evolved at very different rates as well, the former having many millions of years behind it and the latter—linguistic vocalizing—no more than a few million years. The use of symbols has many facets to it (Hockett 1969), some shared with other species, some peculiar to man. To a species that was breaking its bonds to instinctual responses to perceived stimuli as it gained in learned behavior, and as the time lag between receipt of a message and a response to it permitted the exercise of options, the art of symboling, as displayed by the human species, can only be viewed as a quantum leap in evolution.

Signals and symbols

Adaptation, viewed as a state of being, is a measure of the degree to which an individual or a species, represented by both genotype and phenotype, responds successfully to the challenges of an environment. As Slobodkin (1964) so perceptively states it, "the only payoff is the continuation of the game." Among social species, group success is predicated on discipline, whether instinctual or learned; and because apprehension of the environment is mandatory, cohesiveness and fitness of the group requires some form of communication that is communally used. It does not have to be understood in a detailed or conscious sense, but the instructions must be followed. This presupposes that every successful group can generally distinguish in the chaos of incoming information that which is relevant to its survival and can be indifferent to that which is not (Frank 1966). Strategies of existence have been evolved out of such selective awareness.

Signals and symbols are the bases of communication, forms of biological and social economy. To the extent that elements of communication are constant features of an environment essential for survival, to that extent will responses to them be inherited and built into the biogenes; to the extent that they are variable, to that extent must they be learned. But whatever the nature of these incoming messages, an increasingly greater selective value will be placed on the ability to intercept and to interpret them and to make operational those that are relevant.

Signals are instinctual responses to environmental stimuli or fixed expressions of particular emotions and are translated by a receiver and converted into directed behavioral patterns. Signals, therefore, are operators, precise in their evocative content, unambiguous in meaning, and related to the immediate world of being. As a rule, they are directed to a group rather than to a particular individual, although this restriction would hold less for a gestural than a vocal signal. Selective pressure would tend to keep a tight rein on the character of signals, maintaining them discrete, stereotyped, and free of expressive and interpretative nuances. If they were otherwise, they would fail to serve their purpose (Frank 1966). Among nine species of gibbon, for example, the territorial songs and calls are consistent throughout the range of each species, even when that range may be disrupted or overlapping with the ranges of other species, and each signal conveys a specific set of information within, but not beyond, species limits (Marshall and Marshall 1976). Versatility of calls is, therefore, evident in some species of primates, but flexibility of response is less so. Thus, the vervet monkey emits danger signals that distinguish between the presence of a snake, eagle, or lion, but the response among the receivers is invariably appropriate to the particular predator (Seyforth et al. 1980).

Signals can, of course, be gestural as well as vocal. A. H. Schultz, the physical anthropologist, has said, perhaps with tongue in cheek, that "the orgies of noise indulged in especially by howlers, querezas, gibbons, siamiangs, and chimpanzees, seemingly so repetitious and meaningless, are probably at least as informative to the respective species as most after-dinner speaking is to *Homo sapiens*," but he also refers to gestures as "an intricate and voluminous silent vocabulary of great aid in social intercourse."

A signal is an invitation to action, an attention-gaining device, but no interpretation is necessary because the information is embedded in the signal and the response is triggered by the reception. The ability to emit, receive, and interpret a signal is, therefore, generally an inherited and species-specific (racial) phenomenon operating within established constraints, the rigidity of which varies with the species. A knowledgeable bird-watcher needs only to hear a call to be able to distinguish one warbler from another, with the call often being a more certain means of identification than a fleeting glimpse.

Symbols, on the other hand, are a means of dealing not only with a world of knowledge and sensory perception but also with a world of shifting and often transitory shapes and values, where the real and the imagined, the tangible and the illusory, become inextricably interwoven. This has led to an accumulated and infinitely manipulable repertoire of sounds (this is less true for gestures) having no material, temporal, and spatial bounds of meaning. The immediate world of being is only one of many worlds to the symboler. Instead of being stereotyped, the symbol can, if need be, take on an arbitrarily determined significance, invested with no meaning or emotion other than that intended by the symboler and understood by one or more other human beings. More often than not (although less often in the realm of science and mathematics), a symbol takes on a particularity according to the circumstances under which it is used. In addition, a delay can exist between the use of a symbol and a response to it, and this fact provides a time for reflection and interpretation, allows for the separation of emotion and content if both exist, and permits the storage of information for future instead of immediate use. Because a single symbol used by itself may well be devoid of meaningful information, the totality of an image or a concept is generally achieved only by a collection of symbols, arranged in proper sequence and delivered in an appropriate manner to an audience. It is probable that these circumstances led to the origin of grammar and syntax, for they have meanings of their own quite apart from the possible informational content of the symbols themselves.

In order to avoid confusion or misconception, it might be

well to discuss the informational nonequivalency of the nucleotides in DNA and the letters in a written language. It was pointed out earlier in this chapter that a nucleotide possesses a minimal amount of information because a single nucleotide by itself is not translatable into an expressed and useful form. That is, there are only four possible nucleotides—A, T, C, G, or, if thought of in terms of complementary pairs, A–T, T–A, C–G, and G–C—which, if used alone, are capable of yielding only four pieces of information, an amount insufficient to bring any individual of any species to a functional state of expression. If we use the English language as an example, we find that the letters of the alphabet vary in the amount of information contained within them. Thus, the letters *a* and *I*, when used as words, possess a greater amount of information than when used as letters in a word. Also, as Morowitz (1978) points out, infrequently used letters carry more information in them than those more commonly used, since their use narrows the possibilities of meaning and minimizes errors of reception and interpretation. This is a fact recognized intuitively by crossword puzzle addicts, and it has been given quantitative values by the inventor of the word game "Scrabble." Thus, in "Scrabble," the letters *Q* and *Z* are given values of ten, *J* and *X*, values of eight, and all vowels (*Y* is an exception when so used) and the letters *L, N, R, S,* and *T*, values of only one. The twenty-six letters of the English language permit the coining of an almost infinite variety of words of few letters, a variety obtainable in DNA only through an internal arrangement of nucleotide sequences grouped into units of hundreds at a time.

The use of symbols presupposes a sense of self-awareness on the part of the symboler and his audience, a sense of individual identity among others similarly endowed. Symbols are also a reflection of the fact that objects and events have significance peculiar to the individual or to the communal group and of the fact that the human world is arbitrarily invested with meaning and existence with purpose. Frank (1966), in fact, proposes that a value-free nature fostered the creation of symbols and that the shift from signals to symbols may have arisen from a necessity to handle, in a purposeful manner, the more intimately dissectible and variable environment of human society. This, as indicated earlier, is in keeping with the point of view of Jerison (1976), who states that the primitive role of language is that of integration and perception rather than communication and is related to the problem of creating a real and manageable world.

Symbols undoubtedly arose out of the welter of signals of which the noisy primate world is capable. Evolution is too conservative not to have followed the obvious route from signal to symbol, although different regions of the central nervous system would be involved in man as compared to the other related primates. If so, we must suppose that the signal, like the symbol, is also an enabling device, with both being tied to a neural and hence an organic base, but the plasticity of symboling is such as to permit a far more rapid evolution than that based on randomly occurring mutations of biogenes; that is, plasticity of image forming must be matched by plasticity of symboling because the two are intimately related. Our perception of the evolution of the human species rests, consequently, on our knowledge of the dual sources of information making that evolution possible: one inherited and embedded in the DNA of our cells, the other learned, stored, and manipulated as the result of an enormously enlarged central nervous system.

In her book, *Philosophy in a New Key,* in which she deals with the effect and fate of new ideas or new versions of old ideas, Susanne Langer (1957) notes that certain of the ideas seemingly force themselves into the intellectual marketplace and demand immediate recognition, discussion, and, if appropriate, exploitation. She sees as the reason for this forceful entry the fact that these ideas contain within them the promise of resolution of pertinent problems that act as barriers to intellectual or social progress. Further, she sees active and sensitive minds grasping these ideas as they emerge, testing them in as many ways as are possible, stretching their meaning to the limits of flexibility, and eventually incorporating them, with varying degrees of success, into the intellectual structure of a period. Is it unreasonable to suppose that something akin to this, locally, to be sure, and on a much more restricted scale, happened in the early stages of cultural evolution and as a shift was taking place from signaling to symboling?

In seeking to understand the origins of human communicative attributes, however, caution needs to be exercised. As Tanner (1981) has emphasized, the transfer and sharing of environmental and social information are complex phenomena, involving a good deal more than simply a vocal shift from signal to symbol. As studies of chimpanzees have revealed, posture, gesture, body movement, and facial expression join with vocalizing as ways by which information is managed, singly and cooperatively, within a social context. The entire communicative repertoire of the pongid group is required for its members to deal effectively with their environmental and social problems, whereas among human beings these same problems can be dealt with largely by linguistic means. When the shift took place is uncertain, but it is more than likely that the remarkable flexibility of the human language was acquired after, and not prior to, the attainment of a hominoid status. If this is so, our morphological, behavioral, and physiological skills and attributes were developed far in the hominoid past, while our uniqueness as human beings seems to result as much from the evolution of our enabling devices as from the enhancement of our imaging forming abilities.

FOUR

A Further Comparison of Biogenes and Sociogenes

WHEN VIEWED AS A single behavioral phenomenon, culture would seem to represent a new and wholly innovative species character. What species other than our own, for example, exhibits the enormous range of social patterns that can serve to distinguish one culture from another, the repertoire of transmitting devices for individual and group communication, the plasticity of individual behavior and a shifting of roles within the fundamental structure of each culture? But a culture, or culture as a whole, is not a single entity, and when its particulars are examined, many of its basic elements are found to have originated deep within an animal past, at a time when the central nervous system had not experienced the great growth that was to occur in the later stages of human evolution. Most recently, Bonner (1980) has dealt with the beginnings of learning and teaching, elements that are central to the emergence of the human species and that would grow in importance as the brain gradually attained its human dimensions. It was Charles Darwin, in his *Descent of Man* (1871), who drew attention to the many similarities of men, apes, and monkeys, not only in their physical and physiological attributes, but also in those qualities of reason and imagination that would reveal their flexibility and potentiality as both organic and social pressures were brought to bear on them. Darwin would expand his thinking in a subsequent volume, *The Expression of the Emotions in Man and Animals* (1872), to show that those outward manifestations of emotion we think of as more human than animal also find their expression in both wild and domesticated species.

Sociogene versus biogene

What makes culture seem so peculiarly human is due in large part to the remarkably plastic and efficient conceptual, storage and retrieval systems possessed by the human species, reinforced socially by an economical mode of transmission through symboling. It has been postulated here that the conceptual image of an event, object, or idea capable of being transmitted by some kind of enabling device is the basic element, the sociogene, of culture. As such, the sociogene is not a direct derivative of a biogene but is instead the product of the central nervous system. Unlike the biogene, it cannot—at least, not yet—be given a molecular form. A sociogene, consequently, is an abstract informational analogue of a biogene, performing, by means of its own unique enabling devices, an equivalent role in a social context. The two kinds of genes, on the other hand, are related in the sense that the biogenotype has made possible the emergence of sociogenes and sociogenotypes, the latter gaining tangible expression as culture in one of its many forms. Thus, a number of evolving and converging biological features set the stage for the emergence of culture as a behavioral attribute of a protohuman group of primates. Among these features were a tripling of brain size, particularly in the cortical regions, coupled with a more intricate neural circuitry, both of which tended to emphasize retentive, associative, and integrative functions; a growing sense of self-awareness, which brought with it a perceptual sense of separation from an environment and at the same time an active sense of participating social membership; a conceptual capability enabling an individual to carve out from the welter of experience those elements of particular importance to him and to give them an abstract, but still tangible, form that is manageable, transmissible, and shareable; an ability to handle the nuances of symboling so that the species could move from the rigidities of signaling to the plasticity of symboling; and a communal environment that fostered and placed a high premium on the convergence and integration of these features.

It is not sufficient, however, to equate the informational bases of organic and cultural evolution and thereby justify the use of the term *sociogene* as the basic element of cultural evolution. There is no reason to add another term to the literature unless it can be demonstrated that the sociogene shares other attributes with the biogene and thus warrants its identity as well as its informational equivalency. Potter (1964) has previously addressed this problem. He argues "that the processes of natural selection and survival of ideas in cultural evolution are analogous to the natural selection and survival of DNA molecules in biological evolution, and that ideas are the key to understanding cultural evolution just as DNA molecules are the key to understanding biological evolution." Potter's use of the term *analogous* is open to question when it is applied to the evolutionary processes themselves, but the main thrust of his statement is totally in keeping with the arguments presented here. He goes on to state that ideas and DNA molecules—sociogenes and biogenes in the present context—share certain characteristics and capabilities of order and disorder, those elements that provide for the continuity of evolving systems at the same time that they inject sufficient diversity into the systems so that new patterns of adaptation may emerge as the result of selection. Thus, our knowledge tells us that biogenes engage in a number of processes and events, all of which play significant roles in organic evolution: replication; mutation; recombination with other similar elements to provide new patterns of genetic expression; transmission from cell to cell and from generation to generation; expression, sometimes invariably, at other times variably, according to the genetic and physical milieu in which they find themselves; regulation by other biogenes, thus permitting a distinction to be made between structural and regulatory genes; migration and drift into other environments where selection pressures may differ and new genotypes emerge; introgression through hybridization; and oftentimes, extinction through selection or chance. We may then ask whether sociogenes behave in like fashion, or respond similarly to cultural pressures. Those features that are more evolutionary than genetic will be deferred to the last chapter.

Replication of genes

The replication of DNA is a reasonably well understood process. In a competent environment, i.e., in a dividing cell or an appropriately prepared artificial medium, the double helix of DNA opens up and at the termination of the process has replicated itself to form two double helices of identical character. DNA, it should be emphasized, is self-replicating in the sense that it is itself responsible through the expression of its coded information for the cellular mechanisms that guide the replication process from initiation to completion. It is, of course, the complementary nature of its two polynucleotide chains that makes replication possible in the first place. It has been suggested by some that the formation of crystals is a similar kind of replication, but the circumstances are quite different in that the precipitation of crystals is not dependent upon complementarity or upon the presence of a crystal to be copied; indeed, the process may be initiated by an unrelated particle of dust. Neither the replication of DNA nor the formation of crystals is an exact process free of flaw, but DNA reduces its copy-errors to a minimum by error-correcting and heritable enzymes. In this sense, DNA is capable of continuous self-editing as replication goes on.

As a rule, the replication of DNA occurs once during the cell cycle, with the entire mass of DNA being involved. Through this mechanism cells of like genetic constitution, qualitatively and quantitatively, are produced, to add to the mass of a multicellular body or to the number of individuals in the population of a unicellular species. Replication, therefore, is a highly conservative process; like produces like, whether of cells or of individuals, and the species maintains its species-identifying biogenotype. Cells that no longer divide tend to maintain their DNA relatively unchanged throughout their lifetime, although each kind of cell in a multicellular body may be genetically different as well as differentially active, depending on the species, tissue, and patterns of growth and development.

Only in special circumstances does DNA replicate itself partially and selectively. As a rule, failure to replicate leads to the loss of that portion of the biogenotype and all other pieces of DNA attached to it; unreplicated elements of DNA cannot participate successfully in the process of cell division. Chromosome elimination, as a regular part of development or of gamete formation in some species, may be due to such selective patterns of partial replication (Swanson et al. 1981). Overreplication (replicative enhancement) can also occur, most notably in the oocytes of some vertebrates, and it is related to an embryonic need for large amounts of particular gene products.

The sociogenotype that gives to a culture its identifiable characteristics resides in the collective mind of the cultural group as a set of concepts. The conceptual elements of a set may be variously acquired by an individual, but none can be communally shared unless transmitted. Replication and transmission are, therefore, inextricably interwoven in cultural evolution. It is for this reason, it would seem, that Dawkins (1976) identifies this dual-faceted process as one of imitation and his meme as a replicator as well as a unit of cultural transmission or, more concisely, a unit of imitation. Dawkins, it is true, defines imitation rather broadly, but the contention here is that conceptualization and transmission are two quite different processes and that the term *sociogene* is more properly considered to be a product of the conceptualization process. The latter, therefore, has an existence as an entity prior to its transmission. It may be fuzzy or clearly delimited at the time of transmission, and it may even be given definite form during the time of transmission, but the sociogene, nonetheless, has a tem-

TABLE 3   *A comparison of the encoded informational attributes of human bio-genes and sociogenes, using attributes of the former as a basis for examining the nature of the latter.*

Biogenes	Attributes	Sociogenes
1. DNA	Nature	Concepts (ideas)
2. Biparental inheritance via egg and sperm.	Source	Single individuals. Learning reinforced and modified by on-going experience. Parenting and multiparental (social) sources of great initial significance.
3. Molecular by way of gene-directed cellular mechanisms; copy-error low and made more exact by repair mechanisms.	Replication	Oral or inscribed repetition; by way of teaching and hence inseparable from transmission; copy-error high, particularly if oral and because of interpretive differences.
4. Dependent on reproduction. Asexual (somatic): cell to cell by way of replication of DNA, mitosis, and cell division. Sexual: generation to generation by way of meiosis, gamete formation, and fertilization, hence inseparable from recombination. Transmission of biogenes often influenced by cultural practices.	Transmission	Dependent on symboling—words, gestures, signs, etc. Inseparable from replication. Accuracy dependent upon sophistication of both sender and receiver; when inscribed, may transcend both time and place, but copy-error high when oral or gestural, less so as technology for storage and retrieval improved.
5. Dependent on type of reproductive processes: tightness of biogene linkages, segregation of genes and chromosomes, and randomness of gamete union at fertilization.	Recombination	Dependent on size of social group, and amount of contact and intermixing with other groups. Occurs readily in open societies, and is restricted by social authoritarianism, uniform environments, and lack of stressful challenges.
6. Via RNA–protein sequence, coupled with inherited epigenetic rules of growth and development. Affected variously by environmental influences,	Expression	Social phenotypes largely acquired through learning, coupled with an undetermined amount of inherited influence. Varied according to rigidity or flexibility of social environment. Easily

and manifest as morphological, physiological, and behavioral traits.		altered by individual choice stemming from plasticity of interpretation and behavioral expression.
7. Biogene stability high but variable from gene to gene. Occurrence random and unpredictable, and due to nucleotide or chromosomal gain, loss, or rearrangement. Fate determined by selection processes or chance, but heterogeneity of individuals in population indicates that retention is high.	Mutation	Rate of change very high, nonrandom, and may be purposeful. Easily affected by experience, vagaries of interpretation, imaginative manipulation, and social authority. Rate decreases by institutionalization or ritualization of concepts.
8. Occurs most readily at periphery of range and in specialized environmental circumstances. May be random, as with most blood groups, or determined by cultural practices, as with patterns of disease resistance.	Migration and genetic drift	Deliberate borrowing or less deliberate diffusion from other social groups; involves awareness and an assessment of concepts for possible use. Fixation higher the smaller the group.
9. Involves coming to terms with physical environment. Related to breeding structure, environmental variance, effect on adaptation, and retention for a sufficient length of time to permit selective processes to act.	Selection	Involves coming to terms with social environment. Generally deliberate, involving levels of awareness, acceptance, satisfaction, and social appropriateness. Influenced by flexibility of individual choices. Can run counter in being maladaptive, but generally social and natural selections are in harmony with each other.

Note: Evolution involves the temporary and provisional establishment of order out of the available raw materials of disorder (diversity). Among the elements of order in organic evolution are the stability of DNA as a double helix; the precision of its replication, with copy-error minimized by the presence of repair mechanisms; predictable phenotypes based on inherited gene-directed pathways of transcription, translation, growth, and development; reproductive isolation; and physiological stability based on interlocking homeostatic mechanisms. Organic diversity stems from the mutation and recombination of both biogenes and chromosomes, with selection operating on the diverse phenotypes which make their appearance. Migration, genetic drift, and the availability and diversity of environmental opportunities contribute to the establishment of genetically different populations. In cultural evolution, order arises out of a social environment in which concepts needed for social integration are more or less fixed by exposure of the individual to these concepts at an authority-accepting stage, the institutionalization of those concepts necessary for social identity and integrity, and the constant reshaping in the individual of the early acquired attributes through subsequent experience. All other attributes of sociogenes are highly labile, leading to enormous diversity of expression, shifting cultural values and traits, and rapid evolution. The diversity and availability of extrasomatic sources of energy contribute significantly to the rapidity of cultural change. Consult Cavalli-Sforza and Feldman (1981) and Lumsden and Wilson (1981) for additional details and opinions.

poral priority even as DNA precedes the RNAs in the decoding of organic information (this statement holds for multicellular species but may not be correct for the early stages of the origin of life, and it is not true for certain RNA viruses).

No one of us receives and processes unselected and raw data to be turned into mental concepts. The mind's eye of an individual has its own peculiarly ground lenses, with or without aberrations, which on a selective basis admit, refine, integrate, or reject incoming messages (Boulding 1956). It is only when such selected fragments of information, acquired largely in a social context, are given meaningful shape as concepts that they have the possibility of becoming a part of the sociogenotype either of the individual or of the social group as a whole. In a sense, these units are the distillations of experience and memory from which we construct our social uniqueness. It is the mind, the product of the central nervous system, that has the faculty of creating images as well as the symbols needed to define and delimit these images and to thus transform them into transmissible sociogenes. Mathematics would be the ultimate refinement of conceptual and creative symbolism and, at the higher levels of mathematics, the symbol may well become its own reality, transgressing the limits of experiential, but not of imaginative, reality.

Mutability of genes

Biogenes and sociogenes are, therefore, units of information that can be replicated and transmitted time and again. When successful, this ensures the continuity and survival of the species and the culture. Evolution, however, is dependent on diversity, and this in turn depends upon the degree of fidelity with which each kind of gene is replicated, transmitted, and incorporated into their respective genotypes. Each biogene seems to have its own intrinsic degree of instability under reasonably normal environmental circumstances. This is generally referred to as its spontaneous rate of change, which really means that the cause of change or mutation is unknown even if the rate of change can be detected experimentally with considerable accuracy. Thus, certain biogenes in human populations mutate at specific rates: for example, those governing the expression of albinism mutate at a rate of approximately thirty per one million genes; muscular dystrophy at a rate of sixty-seven per one million genes; and classical hemophilia at a rate of about forty-four per one million genes. For reasons that are not entirely clear, bacteria and viruses have mutation rates that tend to be very much lower, on the order of one per one million genes to one per one billion genes. There may well be human genes that mutate at these lower rates, but if so their frequency would be difficult to detect with any degree of accuracy.

Mutations are due, of course, to faulty copying or to environmental insults that damage the DNA. In the case of biogenes, mutations may be unrelated to replication. Thus, ionizing and photochemical radiations and a broad array of specific chemicals can induce both genic and chromosomal mutations, although their altered state may remain undetected until the processes of transcription and translation lead to altered phenotypes. Some mutations are neutral in the sense that they have no effect on the phenotype, but their presence can now be detected if their expression results in an amino acid change in an unimpaired protein.

As might well be expected, sociogenes are far more mutable than even the most mutable of biogenes; their very abstract nature makes them especially vulnerable to change. Even in the mind of the originator, subsequent acts of experience as well as the processes of association, integration, and reflection can give a sociogene a new shape and thus alter its ultimate expression. But the vulnerability of the sociogene to change is most evident during the process of transmission, particularly during the early stages of its existence. Symbols are notoriously slippery elements, for their meaning can undergo change as well; and when one adds to this the fact that the receiver on the transmission end of the replicative process must not only receive but also interpret and integrate as well, copy-error is unavoidably high. The experience and mental capability of both transmitter and receiver are crucial at this stage of reception. Copy-error is minimized only when a sociogene, a concept, is codified by a rigid symbol. Thus, the mathematical concept of zero is represented, in literate cultures, by the letter O and an unknown by the letter X, and their meaning is unmistakable. In other instances, codification may come about by the institutionalization of dogma, accompanied by specific ritualization on the part of selected members of the group; error is reduced by reducing the number and increasing the reliability of transmitters.

Transmission of sociogenes

In the early stages of a culture, the elders of the tribe were the transmitters of those sociogenes that were the basis of tribal identity and continuity. These might be thought of as the source of the control mechanisms of Geertz (1966). The passage of these concepts from individual to individual, and from generation to generation, was rigidly prescribed, and the place of, and respect accorded, the elders reinforced this rigidity. Oral transmission, however, is much subject to error, but when it is the only means for the replication and transmission of sociogenes, the symbols are almost signallike in their invariance; they are taken at face value with a minimum of individual interpretation, particularly if received at an authority-accepting stage of cognitive development. The art of pictography and writing, as well as the modern means of storage, retrieval, and transmission, reduced the amount of mutational error; but interpretative vagaries are a human hallmark, and time and place are not without significance. Nevertheless, any group, primitive or otherwise, has an intuitive respect for stability of or for adherence to form as being of primary importance for survival or identity. Would this correspond to the stabilizing influences of organic evolution? The individual, in essence, confers or gives up a portion of his liberty to a higher social authority, willingly or unwillingly, consciously or unconsciously: to codes of law, systems of governance, the educational system, the religious establishment, caste system, hierarchical levels of privilege or prestige (human pecking order), and so on. The complexity of culture increases the need for these homeostatic mechanisms in much the same manner as their analogues occur in organic systems. The interpretative capabilities of the individual may well be curtailed by this process; it is the price the individual pays for social membership and associated security. But the curtailment is not complete. The individual remains the source of all mutations of sociogenes as he is of biogenes; the same holds true for all new genes as well.

The evolutionary effect of this transfer of control on culture is twofold. For the cultural group, mutations or new sociogenes which impinge on or threaten its deep-seated character (Geertz's control mechanisms?) tend to become dampened or subordinated to the overall problems of persistence and the maintenance of the status quo (Ashby 1960). The new is always a threat to the even tenor of a society, and Lumsden and Wilson (1981) would say, in effect, that this is a way of keeping cultural change on a leash. For the individual, however, a loss of freedom of choice in some matters is counterbalanced by an enhanced freedom in others. Thus, the individual is freed from an immense amount of decision making by being provided with a set of expectations about which little mental consideration needs be given; these expectations, often acquired early in life, become entrained and incorporated into the sociogenotype of the individual, to be expressed as a part, and probably a large part, of his sociophenotype. The enhanced freedom of the individual relates to aspects of conceptual thought less essential for social persistence but which, as Cannon (1939) insists, are the essence of humanity and humanness. It is this freedom, on the other hand, that is the source of diversity on which evolution depends.

Appropriateness of the sociogene concept

The extreme difference in "mutability" between sociogenes and biogenes inevitably raises the question of the usefulness of the sociogene concept. The difficulties of sharp definition are obvious and readily admitted, but if the fuzziness of the sociogene causes one to doubt its reality, one need only be reminded that it has not always been possible to characterize the biogene in as definitive a manner as we can today. Thus, in the mid-1950s, and before the full impact of the molecular nature of the biogene had been felt, L. J. Stadler (1954), a leading geneticist of his day, had this to say about genes:

The properties of the gene may be inferred only from the results of their action ... our concept of the gene is entirely dependent upon the occurrence of gene mutations ... any definition of a gene mutation presupposes a definition of a gene.... The gene cannot be defined as a single molecule, because we have no experimental operations that can be applied in actual cases to determine whether or not a given gene is a single molecule. It cannot be defined as an indivisible unit, because, although our definition provides that we will recognize as separate genes any determiners actually separated by crossing over or translocation, there is no experimental operation that can prove that further separation is impossible. For similar reasons, it cannot be defined as a unit of reproduction or the unit of action of the gene string, nor can it be shown to be delimited from neighboring genes by definite boundaries.

Because of the abstract nature of the sociogene, it is possible that its boundaries, shape, and action will always remain elusively fluid and will never be as sharply delineated as those of the physical biogene. There is no question that we will always encounter these difficulties with such mutable value concepts as love, generosity, altruism, and morality, and even more difficulties with such intangibles as beauty or proportion. But we would find it equally difficult to deny their existence, their cultural significance, and in some instances their adaptive value. In a similar vein, it might also be pointed out that some physical theories are based on the concept of a perfect gas, an idealized situation that is probably never realized but whose centrality to physical thought is critical.

Origin of Sociogenes

The individual has been postulated as the source of new sociogenes or mutated pre-existing ones. This is true for biogenes as well, but, as any geneticist is aware, it is not always easy to determine whether a phenotypic expression in an individual is genic or environmental in origin. The problem becomes even more intractable when, in the human area of expression, one tries to deal with the origins of social behavior or with levels of intelligence and patterns of personality (see Cloninger and Yokoyama's review [1981] of Lumsden and Wilson [1981]). Indeed, the tracking of a human phenotypic expression back to its genic source may well end up in either the bio- or the sociogenotype, or in both if the organic and cultural systems coevolve with reinforcing or complementary interaction.

To return to biogenes, it is probably correct to say that they do not arise de novo, although the introduction of a new gene from external sources, via a plasmid or viral carrier or by introgression, is always a possibility. Can the same be said of sociogenes? Here we are on shifting sands. But it seems most likely that every sociogene also has antecedents, for how can one handle mentally that which is unimaginable or is unrelated to experiential involvement. The sociogene, therefore, as nearly as one can define it at the present time, arises from an act of experience, real or imagined. How then does an act of experience become transformed into a recognizable sociogene, shareable and transmissible? How is the substance of internally generated ideas shaped into concepts with their form and content so delimited that they can be described, managed, and acted upon in a social context? The constraints of the sociogenotype will determine the reception of new genetic elements; this is the area of cognition and of cognitive development, and possibly of the operation of Lumsden and Wilson's (1981) epigenetic rules of coevolution. Information transfer systems must also be involved, for the generator and the receiver of a sociogene must be on a reasonably comparable footing. Assuming that the sensory and neural organs are appropriate to the task, one must further assume that the mind of the individual, or the communal mind, has been sufficiently prepared so that relevant and penetrating acts of experience can be received and stored for either immediate or future use. The interpretation of messages and their integration into the substratum of the mind must occur and, in the human species, be accompanied by a sense of self and time and place, i.e., of social awareness; but it is relevance that will separate the act of experience from the background noise of everyday existence and provide the impetus to give it the necessary shape, content, and texture it must have to be fitted into the conceptual structure of an individual's consciousness. To a considerable degree, these factors have also been shown to be a part of the sensory and mental capabilities of the higher primates and are not, therefore, unique to the human species. But what is unique to human culture is the social necessity of inserting its sociogenes in the scheme of things real or imagined, and of achieving this end by abstract means; i.e., dissecting the physical, social, and mental environment into manageable units, labeling them with arbitrary terms, juggling them until they fit into higher categories of conceptuality, and then deliberately devising a means of information transfer so that they can be shared with others. In the process, the sociogene attains a recognizable and heritable form when the image, individually perceived, is, by reflection and manipulation, elevated to a conceptual level, in which form it can be released into the social environment where its adaptive relevance can be judged, acted upon, rejected, or integrated into the sociogenotype.

Images, of course, vary in their degree of relevance and so, too, do concepts and, hence, sociogenes. The situation is no different in kind from that relating to biogenes. The latter are of many degrees of developmental and evolutionary importance: structural genes which may vary in influence from those that are central for the maintenance of life to those that act on terminal events to provide minor patterns of diversity; regulatory genes which govern the timing and magnitude of action of structural genes; genes that have quantitative as well as qualitative effects; genes that are neutral in effect instead of being deleterious or beneficial; and even stretches of DNA that have no known genetic significance. We can suppose that sociogenes are equally variable in their significance. All can be replicated

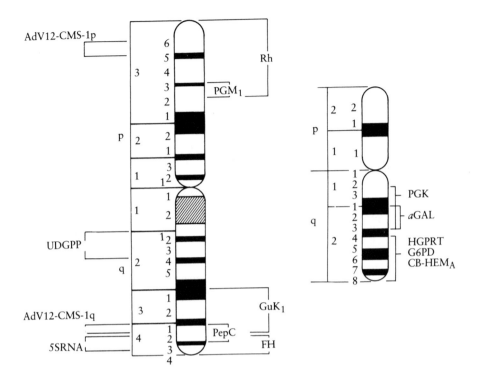

FIGURE 23   *The banded structure and gene locations in chromosome 1 (left) and the X chromosome (right) of man. Chromosome 1 is the longest one in man, and the Rh factor gene is known to be located near the end of the short arm (p); a very large number of genes are known to be located in the X chromosome (the symbols are the acronyms for specific genes, which can be located by a variety of techniques). The banded structure of the chromosomes is the result of special staining procedures, making it possible to distinguish one chromosome from another (see Swanson et al. 1981 for details).*

and carried along in the genotype; all can be mutated or lost as well. And, as Dawkins (1976) has said, genes of whatever sort can be grouped into higher levels and categories of organization, to give rise to coadapted constellations of genes in both the organic and cultural spheres.

To return to the question of mutability again, we can inquire as to the existence among sociogenes of alleles comparable to those known among biogenes. It was the existence of alleles of contrasting sort that led to the development of the science of genetics and then to the identity, location, and laws of transmission of specific genes related to specific traits. Allelic variation is no longer a necessary requirement for the discovery of a particular structural gene; the presence of a specific protein is evidence of the presence of a structural gene in a genome. However, regulatory genes are not so easily identified and characterized, and it might well be that these are far more numerous than are those of a structural type.

The extreme mutability of sociogenes should give rise to innumerable allelic forms, and the field of religion can provide us with such examples. The basic concept of supernatural beings or forces that have an influence on the affairs of human beings has been the source of many forms of polytheism and monotheism, as well as such pseudosciences as astrology. Christianity, for example, is a socioallele of a basic mythological sociogene. Protestantism, with its doctrine of individual versus central scriptural interpretation of sacred writings, is an allele of Christianity; and the vagaries of interpretation being what they are, Protestantism has its own built-in mutagens which have produced a wealth of thematic variations. In the realm of science, however, there is a strong tendency to reduce the allelism of its sociogenes to as low a level as possible, with the ultimate goal of sharply delimiting their dimensions by invariant mathematical symbols. Thus, Boyle's laws, or the factors in the Einsteinian equation $E = mc^2$ are not only economical conceptual expressions of content but are also rigorously constraining as to interpretation. But whatever the nature of a sociogene, its function is to assist us to define the world around us. In the process of doing so, it also gains expression through our behavior, that is, our sociophenotype.

Recombination and segregation of genes

A further source of variation in both organic and cultural systems stems from the recombination and segregation of their respective basic elements. This is a topic dealt with in great detail by Cavalli-Sforza and Feldman (1981) and others, so that only a brief consideration is warranted at this time. In biological systems other than those of a haploid nature, mutation rates alone are far too low to provide the varied phenotypes that are fed into the evolutionary process, and on which selection acts, but the retention of a vast number of mostly recessive mutants in a heterozygous state within the gene pool allows for the emergence of varying genotypic combinations as gamete formation and fertilization link the generations together. Mutation rates of thirty or forty per million genes, occurring randomly in time and place, have been judged by population geneticists to be inadequate to account for the rates of evolution, but if one considers the fact that each human individual possesses a minimum of 10,000 genes, each one of which can exist in various allelic states, the extensive heterozygosity of the genotype is assured. This assumption has been tested and found to hold in a great many species, and there is no reason for excluding the human species from this generalization. This point can be made more concrete by considering that each human being has forty-six chromosomes in each of his cells, with half that number coming from one parent, the other half from the other parent. Each egg and sperm, ready for fertilization, would possess only twenty-three chromosomes, each one of which is highly likely to have at least one gene that differs allelically from its homologous counterpart. Each individual at sexual maturity is capable, therefore, of producing a minimum of over 8 million (2^{23}) eggs or sperm that differ allelically among themselves. Since the other parent has a similar potential for forming genetically diverse gametes, it is unlikely that two independently produced siblings will share the same genetic likeness. Recombination, or crossing over, between members of each pair of chromosomes in the sex cells further increases the prospects of diversity among gametes and hence among the members of a population. Nevertheless, the diversity among human beings is not so great as to produce surviving offspring whose phenotypes place them beyond the pale of human dimensions. There must, as a consequence, be stabilizing influences in the form of inherited patterns, coupled with selection pressures, that tend to keep organic diversity within specific bounds and to maintain that kind of integration and integrity that are the hallmarks of any species, human or otherwise.

In their detailed examination of cultural transmission, Cavalli-Sforza and Feldman (1981) classify organic transmission as strictly *vertical,* i.e., passing from parents to offspring. The rigidity of the epigenetic rules of biological development will guide the formation of the individual from a fertilized egg to its mature form. Cultural transmission and the integration of an individual into a cultural setting provide a far more diverse set of circumstances, and with many factors having an influence on the course of an individual's life in a much less predetermined manner. The term *brainwashing,* now in common use, denotes a form of artificially applied "mutagen" that can significantly alter the sociogenotype even after it has been fully formed and matured. In the early stages of the introduction of an offspring into a culture, the transmission is similarly vertical from parents to offspring, even to the point of being somewhat entrained, but with the difference that the interplay of inherited and learned behavior (i.e., the interplay of temperament and environment) in determining the sociophenotype of the individual is much less precise. In the context of the approach of Lumsden and Wilson (1981), the epigenetic rules of cultural development exert a less constraining influence, and the final expression of social character is far less predetermined or predictable.

The possibilities of a more varied cultural expression among the members of a group are further enhanced by the horizontal nature of cultural transmission, as well as by the fact that the cultural system is a far more open-ended one than is its organic counterpart. It also becomes more open-ended and, hence, less determinate as the individual matures and as its central nervous system comes to exercise its intellectual options, even to the point of transcending its organic origins and acquiring a character of its own. Within the culture, horizontal transmission can involve the social group in part or in its entirety; it can include age groups, peer groups, and authority figures in one area of culture or another, and can even include the past generations through the medium of tribal lore, traditions, customs, and educational exposure. The in-house aspects, inculcated into the young, may be viewed as the conservative elements of cultural transmission, tending to preserve the status quo; the far more precise replication and transmission of DNA molecules are their organic counterparts.

Cultural evolution, however, is likely to be slow if it remains dependent on intracultural influences alone. The million or more years that it took to transform a crudely flaked stone into a polished axe head of good proportion can be attributed in part to a lack of influx of other ideas, as well as to the inertia of change typical of small isolated groups. So it is from sources external to the cultural group that influences capable of transforming the culture are likely to have their origin. Quite independent of major disturbances in the physical environment which can, of course, exert significant selection pressures on both the bio- and sociogenotypes, external sources can contribute conceptual material to complement, modify, or displace those derived from internal sources and thereby can add to, replace, or alter the sociogenotype in any number of ways. Sociogenes of a wholly foreign nature may also be introduced, some of which may be comfortably and readily incorporated into the cultural genotype as a whole, while others, if incorporated, may shake and even cause to be shattered the entire integrative fabric of a prevalent sociogenotype, from the fragments of which a new cultural structure must be formed if survival and persistence is to be sustained. Injected into the cultural scene, these introduced elements are often less important for the specific contributions they make than they are for the disruptive action they have on the entire sociogenotype. Even great cultures are not immune to such "mutagenic" influences. As George Woodberry, an early twentieth-century essayist, expressed it in the magazine *Torch* (1905), cultures tend

to disappear in the surrounding ideas of men. . . . So Athens dissolved like a pearl in the cup of the Mediterranean, and Rome in the cup of

Europe, and Judaea in the cup of the Universal Communion. . . . Always some great culture is dying to enrich the soil of new harvests, some civilization is crumbling to rubbish to be the hill of a more beautiful city, some race is spending itself that a lower and more barbarous world may inherit its stored treasure house. . . . In the extinction of religions, in imperial revolutions, in the bloody conflict of ideas, there is one thing found stable; it is the mind itself growing through the ages. That which in its continuity we call the human spirit, abides.

Introgression or diffusion of genes

Others have dealt far more extensively with the migration or intrusion of ideas from one culture to another; mention might be made here of one such instance as a means of illustration. This is the phenomenon of *introgression,* a term introduced by Anderson (1949) to describe the flow of biogenes from one species to another. Sexual compatibility to some degree between the species is a necessary feature if introgression is to take place, but the flow of genes depends on hybridization followed by backcrossing of the hybrid to one parent or the other. New constellations of biogenes tend to arise, with the expressed phenotypes falling between, and often overlapping, those of the parents. In the end both parental species may lose their distinct identities if they are very restricted in distribution, but the more likely possibility is that incipient species may arise to follow their own evolutionary pathways.

Plant and animal breeders have made effective use of the process of introgression in their search for improved domesticated varieties, with both intra- and interspecific hybridization serving to transfer genes from one source to another. Triticale, for example, is a commercially important hybrid produced by crossing strains of wheat (Triticum) with those of rye (Secale); it exhibits some of the desirable features of both genera. In a cultural sense, introgression is most nearly equivalent to the borrowing or diffusion of ideas or techniques; the former is a more active process of acquisition, but both can be profound in their ultimate effect. The breeder, practicing a rigorous artificial selection, can confine the transfer of genes down to single units, but it is unlikely that so selective a process occurs between cultures; that is, a more likely result is the transfer of a group of ideas or concepts. The effect of the Western impact on Eskimo culture is an example. There is the obvious substitution of the rifle and the snowmobile for the harpoon and the dog-sled; far more subtle yet more devastating in its consequences is the substitution of concepts and the alteration of expectations that threaten the fundamental basis of the culture—its mythology, its interactions with the environment, its mobility, and its diet, for example. Further, the rapidity of change leads to a profound alteration of values. The retention of the old ways of life, which in a more hostile environment served the culture for centuries in a highly adaptive manner, are now left to the elders of the tribe, and to the poets and the artists, performing, in such instances, holding operations at best.

Science also provides us with examples of the diffusion of ideas. The Darwinian theory of evolution through natural selection is not confined in its import to the organic world, as indeed this volume tries to point out. This theory is a sociogene of such power and persuasion as to have convulsed the Western world when it appeared; no intellectual facet would be unaffected, for it invaded and altered the religious, economic, and social spheres as well as changing the entire science of biology. It swept away such well-established sociogenes as the idea of the great chain of being that had its origin in Aristotelian thought, the doctrine of special creation, and the thought that miracles not conforming to the laws of nature were possible. In doing so the theory gave to things and events a historical parameter and a sense of their relation to the flowing of time; transience was substituted for the eternal verities. In an equally profound sense, the elucidation of the structure, behavior, and informational potential of the DNA molecule—developed conceptually into what might almost be considered a super sociogene—has once again restructured the science of biology, this time by providing an outlook and a philosophy that would lessen the distinctions that separated biology from the related sciences of physics and chemistry on the one hand, and those of psychology and sociology on the other. In the process, a common basis of inheritance would be established for all organisms from viruses and bacteria to man, and at the other extreme techniques would be developed that permitted the transfer of genes between species of quite different taxonomic categories and which bid fair to alter significantly the science and art of medicine, as well as our views of the substance of human nature.

Not all sociogenes undergo introgression so readily or are so deeply pervasive in their effect. The sociogenotype of a culture may bar or facilitate the entry and integration of a sociogene, or it may tolerate its presence with equanimity. I am reminded of a scene I chanced to witness in a small cathedral in one of the Latin cities of South America. A priest whose features revealed his Indian ancestry was carrying out his priestly duties in the company of his fellow priests, after which he moved to a small, relatively unadorned altar situated some distance away at the side of the cathedral. Here he appeared to be performing a number of acts that seemed to depart strangely from the usual repertoire of Christian rituals. Upon inquiry as to their meaning, I was informed that he was "making his peace with his Indian gods."

FIVE

Organic and Cultural Evolution

The basic similarity of evolving systems

ALL FORMS OF evolution, from the cosmic to the cultural,
are fundamentally similar processes. Each new one arises as an
offshoot from its immediate parent process when the circumstances in one portion of the evolving system—environmental
or organismic—become sufficiently and appropriately unique
and dominant to force a shift away from the main direction of
evolutionary flow. The reason for any given shift may be difficult to detect or understand, but something must obviously free
one part of a system from its directional constraints to allow it
to evolve and participate in another line of development. Each
such thrust is a foray into new and untested territory, a probing
the success of which would depend upon new sets of interacting features. Not all such forays would, of course, be successful; indeed, the majority would be unlikely to persist for a
length of time sufficient to consolidate any gains and to establish the levels of stability needed to meet the new challenges encountered. On the other hand, the occasional and successful
combination of factors would, in time, lead to a reshaping or a
regrouping of past structures and processes, and eventually to
the emergence of new forms of order, exhibiting different patterns of information and constraints and different phenotypic
expressions. In a fundamental sense, therefore, each new thrust

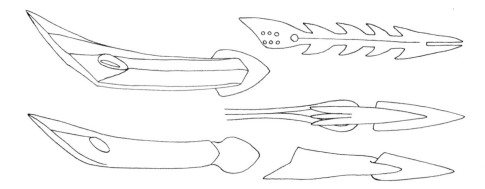

FIGURE 24   *Various toggle-type (left) and toggle-and-barb type (right) harpoons made and used by the Eskimos for hunting whale and seals in Arctic waters. The tips are of slate, bone, or shell, all native materials, and fastened into wooden shafts. These would be abruptly replaced by the rifle, even as the dog sled was replaced by the snowmobile, giving the Eskimos greater success in hunting and greater security in a harsh and hostile environment. The whole concept of hunting, and the relations of animals to man, would undergo significant change and would have a ripple effect that would affect the entire cultural structure.*

results as much from a shift in emphasis in, and importance of, the basic element(s) subject to selective pressures as it does from the pool of existing diversity in that area; that is, new phenotypes may result from a variety of basic regulatory changes: from variations in the performance of control mechanisms, or from altered emphases on particular physiological processes, and not necessarily from any new structural or biochemical features. Eventually the critical selection forces would come to differ from those operating on the evolving elements underlying change in the past and would tend to push the emerging phenotypic expression in different directions from that pursued by the parental process.

Each newly arisen system would retain a feature that is seen in all evolving circumstances, that is, a gradual transformation of simpler systems into ones of ever-increasing complexity.

With the hindsight that comes from consciousness of self, a knowledge of the environment, and the ability to perceive the course of certain processes evolving through time, we can see that from among the possibilities present in the cosmic system, it would be a planet of a particular size, located in a solar system of a particular age, temperature, and dimension, and circling its sun at a particular distance, that would become the stage for a particular kind of evolution based on the carbon atom. Out of this would emerge a highly stable molecule able to draw on the environment for material and energy as it came to acquire its replicative capabilities. It is not known with certainty at what point in the course of organic evolution DNA came to have its present molecular and informational form, but cellular life would come into existence when this replicating molecule became encased in a membrane that would isolate the inner contents from the exterior environment while allowing for the passage of appropriate materials in and out of the cell. A good deal of selectivity was involved in this process, for life is based to a large extent on right-handed sugars and left-handed amino acids even though their mirror counterparts were present at the same time and could have served equally well. And finally, many millions of years later and from among the multitude of organs and processes exhibited by living things, the pattern of encephalization would become selectively emphasized, leading to the development of an enlarging central nervous system and making possible, in the primate group of vertebrates, the emergence of a faculty for enhanced conceptual imagery. Coupled with these changes would be an equally important means for externalizing these images so that they could be shared communally. All of these changes would, of course, be accompanied by a multitude of other supportive and evolving phenomena to make possible the emergence of the human species. That is, the central nervous system's evolution would be pointless unless related systems gave it a frame of organic reference within which its selective potential could be expressed.

It is thus being argued that cultural evolution is not simply an analogue of organic evolution, as many anthropologists and biologists have maintained. More accurately, it is a form of organic evolution striking out in a new and different direction and bringing into existence qualities and phenomena that are also new and different. This branching is, in principle, no different from that which led to the formation of galaxies and solar systems, to the origin of living systems from inanimate circumstances, or to the invasion of land by a previously restricted aquatic group of animals. It was by "tinkering" with specific features of a protohuman assemblage of organisms that evolution would bring into being a number of modified but coordinately intermeshed structures whose collective action would be expressed as the type of behavior that can conveniently be embraced by the generic term "culture." Culture, like history, represents "the self-consciousness of mankind," every aspect of which started out as the outward expression of some thinking human being (Shklar 1980).

From its earliest beginnings, those aspects of culture which would come to be characteristic of the human species would acquire an autocatalytic and rapidly assertive nature, bursting into the vertebrate and primate world with unprecedented speed during the Pleistocene. They would have their own patterns and rates of change, with their own basic evolving elements and modes of expression, and be subjected to different selective pressures. In the process, the instinctual and inherited action-and-reaction behavior of less advanced species of primates would become replaced, in large part, by increased learning capacities and by an enhanced sense of anticipation for guiding "choice of strategies" as goals, needs, and the exercise of freedom became a part of continued existence (Bennett 1976).

The emerging forms were thereby endowed with a second mode of inheritance to complement that conferred on them by their sexually acquired biogenes. Selection pressures for continued adaptation would tend to shift from the physical and physiological features to those of a more psychological and social nature. A slackening of pressures for morphological change would occur as the enhancement of mental faculties, exemplified by an improvement in conceptual, communicative, and technological abilities, would offset the need for any further specialization of organic structures. This does not imply that organic evolution has ceased, but there is no doubt that it is subordinate to cultural evolution as a molding force in human societies.

Evolutionary patterns

Given the initial existence of the force of gravitation acting on the cosmic debris resulting from the big bang, the events leading up to the emergence of human culture almost seem, in retrospect, to have an element of inevitability about them; that is, when one event instead of another occurs or is selected for, it is bound to affect that which happens subsequently. To speak of an inevitability, however, is to invite a metaphysical interpretation, and no such intent is implied. In an evolving and unstable universe, each moment in time contains an element of novelty. Because the character of the novelty is unpredictable, the effect of that novelty on the direction of change is equally unpredictable; but each event that occurs tends to have a focusing effect, setting the stage for that which follows and, indeed, placing constraints on what is subsequently possible. It is just that not all things are evolutionarily possible, and a certain amount of channeling, determined by past events, will inevitably take place. Further, an inherited "blueprint" cannot be scrapped and a fresh start made; evolution makes do with what is available, and evolutionary events are historical, unique, and irreversible. Culture arose, therefore, like any other behavioral change, because of the options available at the time, and not because the options were ideal. Many an engineer, viewing the human body, and many a self-appointed messiah, appraising human behavior, have come up with what they believe to be better designs for human form and action; but organic evolution is a tinkerer with no foresight, while cultural evolution includes the choice of options rather than the uncertainty of future trends.

At each of the evolutionary branch points, information would become packaged into more and more concentrated and different forms: from the relative lack of information characterizing individual atoms to the increasing amounts of information packaged in the form of molecules, cells, organisms, and cultures, each with its own retrieval or enabling mechanisms for expressing or externalizing that information. Information itself becomes, therefore, a kind of selective force, for when it is packaged within a system it inevitably leaves a trace differing from that which would have been left had some other piece of information been stored in its place. Further, the very act of storage becomes increasingly a factor in subsequent selection. To add or detract anything from the form of an atom is to alter drastically its nature or its information, even if it only involves shifting to an ionic or an isotopic state. As learning enters the organic world to enhance the process of information acquisition, storage depends, in part, upon that which had been previously stored; that is, newly encountered experiences are judged in the light of past experiences. It is through such channeled actions that the process of individualization takes place. That which can be stored depends upon that which previously had been sensed and remembered. It is not possible to escape this individuality, for the slate of experience cannot be wiped clear. We can modify, but it is difficult to forget the past.

Each evolutionary branch is also characterized by its own pattern of acceleration, with each of the several evolving systems proceeding at a rate faster than its predecessor. The kinetics of any process is, of course, determined by the kind and stability of the basic unit involved, as well as by the degree to which it responds to any altering or selective force. In biological and cultural realms, the modes of information packaging, extraction, expression, and transmission may also exert varying effects on rate: the world of instant information in which we now exist cannot fail to have an effect on the world of culture. Each process, at its inception, had its lag period of slow change, followed by a more rapid exponential phase of growth that would increase with time. The appearance and rise of the vertebrates in the Ordivician period and of the mammals in the middle of the Mesozoic era are examples of an expanding growth following a long period of slower incubation. This is true for cultural evolution as well. The transition from a pebble tool, to a crudely flaked axe or knife, to one of beautiful symmetry and surface must have occurred so slowly that from one generation to the next the changes would have been difficult to detect. Even more difficult, undoubtedly, would have been discovering the causes of such directional change. An axe would have been of obvious utilitarian value to its inventor, but what pressure—if such it was—transformed the axe beyond its form of maximum utility to one of sculptural refinement? A sense of proportion would probably have emerged from a feel of kinesthetic balance, but does a sense of aesthetic beauty follow inevitably?

One can assume, with some justification, that toolmaking, as one form of cultural expression, shifted from its slow lag period to one of exponential growth when someone with imaginative foresight conceived of the idea of making a tool for the purpose of making other tools. The shift in conceptual imagery is a profound one because the emphasis moves from present and immediate advantages to those of an indeterminate but possibly more fruitful future.

Evolution and change

The human species like other species is unable to cope with high and continuous levels of change for protracted periods. Chaos, the opposite of order, is the usual result, and with that comes the breakdown of the individual, cultural group, or species. In fact, the human species is probably less tolerant of such change because both its biogenes and its sociogenes may be subject to mutation or environmental impact, with the latter being the more susceptible to change by impinging forces. But as was pointed out before, playing the game of evolution requires uninterrupted and active participation, and to have this requires that there be a constant selection in the direction of stability. The question may, therefore, be raised as to whether cultural systems emulate organic ones in maximizing fitness, or adaptation. Is the exercise of options a cultural equivalent to natural selection? Do homeostatic mechanisms also arise in cultural circumstances to dampen the effects of variation and to enhance the probabilities of survival in the face of environmental challenges? Do the two systems complement each other, or can the evolution of one system be out of phase with that in the other system?

If a more or less permanent alteration in the environment occurs to which the species must adapt if it is to survive and reproduce, the means for coping with that change will gradually be built into the genotype of the species. Random mutations, the raw material of organic evolution, will be acted upon by natural selection, and those that favor survival in the now-altered environment will have a greater tendency to spread to all members of the species and thus to become incorporated into the genotype. Ecotypes of both plant and animal species attest to the sensitivity of genotypes to respond to alterations in the environment. When such groups are analyzed genetically, innumerable small but heritable adjustments are revealed that have brought the ecotypes into better rapport with their local environments. Can it be said that similar trends occur during cultural evolution to bring into being altered sociogenotypes with increased degrees of fitness?

In a confined and stable environment—physical, organic, or social—evolution does not cease; change will occur slowly, but in all probability it will involve the refinement of those traits, heritable or learned, suitable for that situation rather than the introduction of new and different traits. In the organic realm, for example, the brachiopod genus of deep marine waters, Lingula, has undergone relatively little morphological variation since the Paleozoic era, some 475 millions of years ago, while the recent introduction of antibiotics and pesticides into the environment have led to the rapid fixation of different heritable changes in the genotypes of exposed bacterial and insect species.

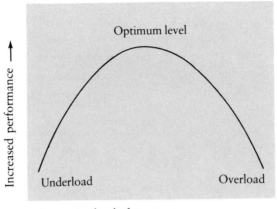

Increasing level of stress ⟶

FIGURE 25

An overload of stress can carry an organism or a species beyond its adaptive level, with ensuing disaster of failure or extinction because the circuitry itself becomes overloaded. Insufficient stress, or underload, can be equally deleterious because the control mechanisms, be they cultural or organic, can be subject to unfortunate change without being aware of the challenge. Physiological and cultural flexibility, of course, permits oscillation between extremes for short periods, and without serious effect. An optimum stress keeps the cultural or organic system "fit" without subjecting it to overloads, or allowing it to go slack because of no stress (modified from Potter 1971).

The dampening of change

In the cultural sphere, the human species can manipulate the physical and social environment for its own ends, and those elements of the sociogenotype that relate most closely to social stability gradually become institutionalized, the cultural equivalent of genetic stabilization. These are judged to be the homeostasis of a culture, those elements that contribute significantly to its form and substance and that set the limits of acceptable individual behavior. In another sense, these sociogenetic phenomena act as the lenses of a culture, focusing the small repetitive aspects of daily life so that the final, collective result transcends the possible achievement of any single member. These are what give philosophical meaning and practical direction to the facts of everyday existence and what help to transform the chaos of experience into a structured and intelligent pattern. Or, to put it otherwise, these contribute to the image a culture has of itself and the world around it, as well as providing the means it invents to span the gap between what is and what might be.

Saint Paul said that to be understood the invisible must be made visible. Today we see some of these homeostatic mechanisms institutionalized into systems of law, more or less dogmatized religions, structured governments, sequential patterns of education, and systematized rituals of initiation into organizations of bewildering variety—churches, Rotary, street gangs, Greek fraternities and sororities, political parties, even the DAR. Many can be traced back to preliterate cultures where their adaptive value must have been different from what it is now, but even today each gives to its initiates a sense of cultural security and solidarity denied to those on the outside. Evolution is at work in each of these systems. The cotillion, once a lively dance but in some sophisticated cultures today a formalized, if outmoded, means of introducing their eligible daughters to adult society, is an evolutionary vestige of a means for coping with a central cultural crisis, i.e., the rites of passage which carried an individual from adolescence to maturity and which made her a participatory and adult member of the culture.

To the extent that institutionalized images are rigidly structured, to that extent is cultural variation in that sector dampened, and evolution slowed. But no two individuals have the same experiences or the same genotypes (identical twins excluded), and messages continually flood in from the environment. So in cultural situations, as in organic ones, the individual is the source of mutations upon which evolution feeds. In earlier times the transmission of cultural change was limited because only selected members of the group were the repositories of tribal lore and because the language chosen to pass on the myths, magic, and heroic deeds of the past was itself formalized and taken at face value. Today we create institutions, cultural "mutagens," as it were, to hasten the rate of change: establishments of research and development and the so-called think tanks. We tend to associate these sources of change with industry or the military, but the virus of change is not so selective. In the world of painting, for example, the human faces of Picasso and DeKooning are far removed from the individualized ones of Rembrandt or Hals, and even more so from the depersonalized but glorified Madonnas of the Middle Ages. The result is that today we scarcely have time to accommodate to that which is new before it is replaced by something even newer. It is little wonder that the future of man will be altered far more profoundly and extensively by cultural evolution than it will be by the very much slower processes of organic evolution.

Institutions, however, have a way of perpetuating themselves to an extent that suggests that they can acquire a life of their own, sometimes well beyond the point of cultural usefulness (the cotillion is an example). Some may even possess a negative selection value. As Dethier (1981) has stated it, "a nervous system [i.e., the source of sociogenes] can transcend its genetic endowment and learn behavior genial to itself, even contrary to the best interest of the gene." The ceremonial contact with dead relatives by means of cannibalism practiced by the Fore tribe of the New Guinea highlands provides them with a sense of continuity with the past, but it is also a means for transmitting the deadly Kuru virus (Cavalli-Sforza and Feldman 1981). Concepts of political, religious, racial, and even military superiority, rife in today's political scene, seem to have equally negative values as far as the adaptability and unity of the human species is concerned, although one must realize that an opposite point of view would be advanced by those who would like to single out their human "socioecotype" and modes of belief as of superior evolutionary significance.

Dawkins (1976) has recognized the difficulties of assigning positive or negative values to any given social phenomenon. He cites the concept of celibacy as a case in point. It would, at face value, seem to possess only a negative selection value since the act precludes the perpetuation of the celibate's genes in the human biogene pool. But if the opposite of celibacy, i.e., marriage and procreation, weakens the power of the priest or nun to influence his or her flock and to propagate the basic teachings of the church, then celibacy can possess a positive adaptive value to a certain segment of culture. This may well be true in the well-established and widespread religions, but the same practice of celibacy spelled the doom of the smaller Shaker sect in this country.

This raises the question of the coevolutionary features of the organic and cultural systems, a topic explored in depth by Lumsden and Wilson (1981). It is obvious that the behavior of any human being (any animal, in fact) possessing a central nervous system is a product of both its heredity and its on-going experience. The contribution of each will vary, of course, with the species, with the cultural looming larger and larger as the primate line evolves. Selection, both natural and cultural, acts on the total phenotype of the species, but it is the contention of Lumsden and Wilson (1981) that human choices among alternative sociogenes (their culturgens) are fixed to a large extent by genetically determined epigenetic rules. The cognitive processing of information is subject to constraints that "channel mental development in specific directions during the interaction between an individual's genotype and environment" (Cloninger and Yokoyama 1981). In other words, the Lumsden-Wilson approach assumes that biogenes influence the probability of acquiring specific sets of sociogenes, and that the coevolution of genes and culture is determined by the existence of two interwoven and interacting sets of epigenetic rules, but with the cultural set dominated by the organic set because it is the latter that establishes the constraints within which the former must operate. The paucity of supportive data and testable approaches leaves the Lumsden-Wilson version of coevolution in a provocative, if tenuous, state. It also raises again, but leaves unanswered for their critics, the old question of whether the "nature versus nurture" problem involves a false or a genuine dichotomy.

Evolution and energy

This comparison of various aspects of organic and cultural evolution will be terminated by dwelling briefly on the role of energy in both systems. The acquisition of appropriate substances and sufficient energy is, of course, a necessary feature of the evolutionary strategy of every species. A species moves in one evolutionary direction or another because of greater opportunities for environmental exploitation, or because of an enhanced ability to acquire materials and energy for its own use. Extinction ensues when the ability to compete is inadequate, or when the resources of the environment are insufficient for continued survival.

The food supply, however intriguing a subject it might be, will not be considered further since it can be assumed that all species require roughly the same substances for maintenance, although the source, form, and amount of food can vary enormously. In the present context, however, energy poses a somewhat different problem because the ability to extract, convert, store, and utilize energy is one of the major factors separating the human species from all other forms of life. The more complex a species, the more successful it is likely to be in managing its energy needs, but the human species has greatly transcended its origins in being able to tap extrasomatic sources unavailable to other species. This is clearly a cultural, not an organic, achievement because it was accomplished through the agency of sociogenes and their derived technology.

Without exception, every activity engaged in by an organism involves an energy requirement or is related to an energy exchange. Since few reactions are 100 percent efficient, with varying amounts of energy being radiated as unreclaimable heat, an organism is an energy transmitter as well as an energy utilizer. The demand for energy replenishment is constant, although it varies in intensity from a basic metabolic level to that at the peak of activity (Hainsworth 1981). As judged by the rates of oxygen consumption, the basic metabolic rate and hence the energy needs will vary widely among different classes

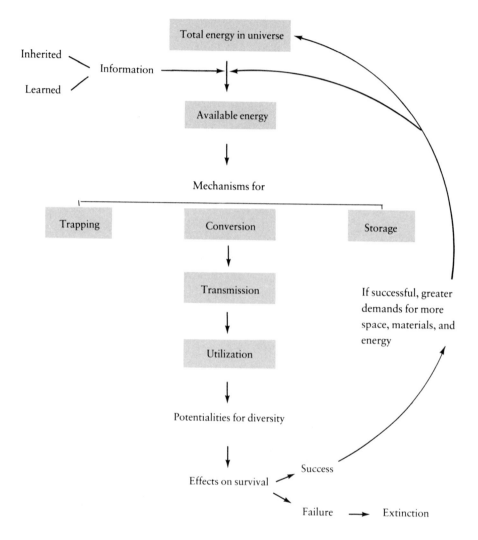

FIGURE 26   *Diagram depicting the flow of energy through a system, and the results of success or failure. Evolutionary change can affect every step in the flow chart. Only organic and cultural evolution have special units—DNA and the central nervous system, respectively—set aside for the management of information critical to the functioning of the system. The human species is distinguished by the degree to which it has been able, through learned information, to increase the amount of available energy.*

of organisms. Among warm-blooded species, for example, the elephant, which weighs more than a million times the tiny shrew, consumes on a per gram basis 100 times less oxygen (Tucker 1975). Man, being a rather large animal, would fall somewhere between these two extremes.

If an organism is to persist, the intake of energy must obviously equal or exceed the outlay of energy required for its capture and utilization. The biological world, in all its varied forms, represents a highly ordered state that would rapidly degenerate into a state of disorder if this ability should cease, as it does when an individual dies. For this reason there must be a constant source of energy available to maintain that order (Morowitz 1978). In any environment there is a specific amount of energy; how much of that is available to a species is a function of the form in which the energy is bound and the ability of a species to extract and convert it for its own use. Management of its energy budget is, consequently, a measure of the success of a species on a daily basis as well as through extended time. For many species, the difference between sufficient and insufficient amounts of needed energy may be narrow indeed. This was true for many of the civilizations of the ancient world as well. Boulding (1964), for example, suggests that the great cities of Sumer and Babylon never had more than a two-week supply of food available, thus making the siege a particularly effective military maneuver. Size has a good deal to do with this. The shrew, as an example, consumes three times its body weight each day to keep its life from being snuffed out as a result of the relatively huge amounts of energy lost through its surface. Even temporary deprivation can be fatal. The hummingbird, with a higher metabolic rate, survives the dusk-to-dawn period by entering a state of torpor, thereby reducing its energy needs at a time when it cannot maintain a high intake level. Large animals, man included, have bodily reserves that can carry them over periods of no or limited intake.

Few animals can supplement their energy needs through the use of extrasomatic devices. Ants may "farm" with aphid "slaves" or may cultivate deliberately certain species of fungi,

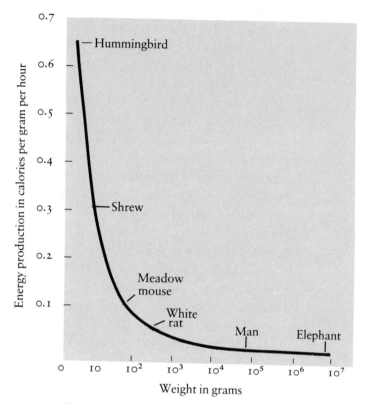

FIGURE 27 *Energy production in mammals as a function of weight. The energy is produced as the food supplies are being burned in the body. The very high rates in hummingbirds and shrews place them in a dangerous position should food supplies fail even for a short period, whereas man and the larger mammals have reserves that they can draw upon and that are consumed at much slower rates. A good deal of flexibility is achieved by such slow rates in man, because it is not necessary to search constantly for food (modified from Gamow 1965).*

and chimpanzees may use stems of grass to extract termites from their tunneled mounds. But these are meager efforts when compared to the means by which the human species has exploited additional energy sources for its own benefit. This is the major reason for its present biological dominance, and the exploitation has taken many forms. The use of tools to supplement its own physical powers is obvious; one need only cite the manner by which weaponry has evolved during the past 2 million or more years, from the stone axe and thrown spear to the intercontinental ballistic missile. Both the effectiveness as well as the range of effectiveness has increased dramatically, moving from a long slow lag period of growth to the exponential growth pattern of recent years. Far more important in its potentiality as well as in its efficiency, however, has been the development of concepts and the invention of a symbolic language to externalize them. Indifference to ideas and to words is profoundly detrimental. The energy of an idea, expressed through language, is not easily calculable, but few can doubt its reality. The phenomenon of displacement illustrates further the interrelation of language and energy. The presence of an object or the enactment of an event is not necessary when language or pictures can convey its sense; the amount of energy conserved increases as the number of listeners increases, while language in its written or electronically transmitted forms has the additional potential of shrinking time and space as well.

The control of fire as the next extrasomatic energy source enabled man to heat his habitation, cook his meals, and ward off the darkness and his enemies, and also moved him from a paleolithic to a bronze and, eventually, to an iron age, giving him increased options for the expression of his growing inventive capabilities. Use of the energy of wind and water would enhance man's mobility and ease the burden of manual tasks, while the tapping of fossil and nuclear energy sources would provide the driving force for the expansion and diversification of cultural expression. Even so seemingly innocuous an invention of the stirrup and the horse collar contributed to the energy budget of the human species (White 1962). They shifted the burden of agricultural labor from the ox to the horse, increased the amount of manageable farm land by one-third, helped to institute a reasonable system of crop rotation, led to a large increase in population, and was responsible for the establishment of the feudal system of governance. In short, their use significantly altered the agricultural, political, social, and military aspects of Europe and the Middle Ages.

However, it is the domestication of plants and animals, which began about 8,000 to 10,000 years ago, that provides us with the most dramatic example of coevolution and of how a cultural adaptation can be a factor in promoting the Darwinian fitness of a species (Cavalli-Sforza and Feldman 1981). Domestication, and particularly those aspects relating to the management of preservable cereals, would lead to a profound shift in a way of life from the hunting and gathering stages to a more stable and sedentary existence; allow for a greater exploitation of the matter and energy of the environment; permit the human species to expand its numbers in explosive fashion; provide the growing population with the nutritional energy for bridging the gap between harvests; and generate the leisure that enabled groups and individuals to initiate and develop those activities that, while possibly only peripheral to mere survival, are the basis of culture and the hallmark of the human race. The central nervous system, freed from total involvement with the problems of survival and reproduction, would unleash culture from its organic base and thus free it to go its own peculiarly human way.

SIX

A Summing Up

As we have tried to trace the evolutionary origins
of the human species, we have come to recognize that these
threads of history extend back to the very beginnings of the
universe, far beyond the origins of life, of our solar system, and
of the planet on which we have our existence. But there are discernible patterns in this history, and pattern follows pattern
without break, from the beginning to the present. We have
come to recognize that it is the nature of the universe to be unstable, that changes occur randomly within patterns, and that
all existing parts of it continue to evolve. As Bateson (1979) has
said, it is an ongoing process that "feeds on the random," an
exploration in the presence of change that leads into the future.
Differences and distinctions of shapes, forms, and relations—
but not necessarily of quantities—make their appearance, and
the new, if it is to persist, must outlive its alternatives. It is a
world that changes constantly and directionally, but not pre-
dictably. Among the various hierarchies of order, some were of
such permanence, and were characterized by such modes of information and energy concentration, utilization, and transformation, that one part of the system—the human species—has
acquired the ability to see things in context, to detect patterns
of change through time, and thus to penetrate its own past, to

visualize itself as part of the whole, and to understand, with a modicum of certainty, that which has taken place. We can now try to answer two of Gauguin's three questions: we think that we know whence we have come and what we are, even if we do not know whither we are going.

Evolution through all time has been a continuous, energy-driven process, although the rates and directions of change have not been uniform within the system. Most variation, at least in the biological world, has been thematic in nature, repetitious but with modulation, which introduces a good deal of diversity but does not drastically alter direction. A number of branch points of an innovative character have arisen, however, and these have been sufficiently distinct in character to be referred to as cosmic, chemical, biological or organic, and cultural. Each branched off from a preceding course of events when a portion of the system achieved a sufficiently different character and level of complexity to cross a critical threshold. It would bring with it the beginnings of a qualitatively unique pattern of expression, a pattern that, as it gained in distinctiveness, would now be responsive to different internal changes and external pressures. New forms of order, constructed out of qualitatively different basic units, would make their appearance. Order is information, and the information contained in each new form of order would be differently packaged, retrieved, and utilized, the energy driving each emerging system would be of another, generally more entropic, character, and the rates of change would be accelerated almost exponentially as each branch established itself. Each system would retain and reflect a memory of its past at the same time that it possessed the potential for future change.

The informational structure of organic evolution came to be based on the double helix of DNA, a remarkable molecule that was not only the repository of coded information for defining an individual exhibiting specific characteristics but was also the possessor of the means for the retrieval of that information for purposes of survival and reproduction. In the animal kingdom, the inherited bank of information would come to be supplemented by a creative process of learning from experience, a process that in the vertebrate line of evolution would be accentuated and accelerated as the mammals, primates, and, eventually, man made their appearance. Bonner (1980) has rightly emphasized learning and teaching as necessary ingredients for the branching off of cultural evolution from its organic base, for they made possible an almost exponential increase in the size of the sociogene pool. Each increase in brain mass was a morphological reflection of this triumph of learning, which can be viewed as a creative replacement for the lessening store of instinctual behavior encoded in the bank of inherited DNA. The individual and the species would, to a degree, be released from the inherited bonds of its past, behavior would tend to take its cues from environmental rather than genotypic sources, and cultural evolution would assume a major role in the molding of the human species.

Coupled with the learning process would be an increased capability for managing the flow of information coming in from the ever-expanding horizons resulting from improved sensory perception and discrimination. There would be an enhanced ability to store information in, and retrieve it from, the memory bank of the mind. In time, human actions would be invested with purpose as a lag period interposed itself between the receipt of information and the response made to it. "In the beginning was the idea" (Bateson 1979), and it came into being as a shift was made from the signal-receipt-response pattern of existence to the signal-receipt-appraisal-integration-storage-or-response pattern, a shift from a predetermined epigenesis to a pattern of creative learning and response. The lag period would provide the opportunity for the exercise of options in the retention and ultimate disposition of such information, with plasticity of behavior accompanying the ability to choose between two or more alternatives. Plasticity of behavior is an inherited phenomenon, but the manner in which that plasticity is used is learned, not inherited. That is, we know of no significant correlation between traits of known genetic origin and those of cultural derivation. This plasticity is by no means peculiar to man, but it achieves its highest expression in the human species, aided, as time passes, by the invention of increasingly sophisticated symbolic and technological enabling devices for the retention and management of that which has been learned. Ideas extracted from this information and shaped into concepts form the creative and informational basis of culture. Collectively, these constitute its "DNA," its sociogenotype, and, as concepts and their expressions are being tinkered with within a social setting, cultural evolution became the latest branching fork along the course of universal evolution.

Bibliography

Anderson, E. 1949. *Introgressive Hybridization.* New York: John Wiley & Sons.

Ashby, W. R. 1960. *Design for a Brain: The Origin of Adaptive Behavior.* New York: John Wiley & Sons.

Barrow, J. D., and J. Silk. 1980. The Structure of the Early Universe. *Sci. Amer.* 242: 118–29.

Bateson, G. 1963. The Role of Somatic Change in Evolution. *Evolution* 17: 529–39.

———. 1979. *Mind and Nature: A Necessary Unity.* New York: E. P. Dutton.

Bennett, J. W. 1976. Anticipation, Adaptation and the Concept of Culture in Anthropology. *Science* 192: 847–52.

Berrill, N. J. 1955. *Man's Emerging Mind.* New York: Dodd, Mead.

Blakemore, C. 1977. *Mechanics of the Mind.* Cambridge: Cambridge Univ. Press.

Blum, H. F. 1963. On the Origin and Evolution of Human Culture. *Amer. Sci.* 51(1): 32–47.

Bonner, J. T. 1980. *The Evolution of Culture in Animals.* Princeton: Princeton Univ. Press.

Boulding, K. 1955. Notes on the Information Concept. *Explorations* 5: 103–12.

———. 1956. *The Image: Knowledge in Life and Society.* Ann Arbor: Univ. of Michigan Press.

———. 1964. *The Meaning of the Twentieth Century.* New York: Harper & Row.

Brace, C. L. 1979. *The Stages of Human Evolution: Human and Cultural Origins.* 2d ed. Englewood Cliffs, N.J.: Prentice-Hall.

Brooks, Van Wyck. 1956. Reflections on the Avant-Garde. *New York Times Book Review,* Dec. 30, 1956, pp. 10–11.

Butzer, K. W. 1980. Civilizations: Organizations or Systems? *Amer. Sci.* 68: 517–23.

Campbell, B. 1966. *Human Evolution: An Introduction to Man's Adaptations.* Chicago: Aldine.

Cannon, W. 1939. *The Wisdom of the Body.* 2d ed. New York: Norton.

Caplan, A. L., ed. 1978. *The Sociobiology Debate: Readings on Ethical and Scientific Issues.* New York: Harper & Row.

Carr, A. 1967. *So Excellent a Fishe.* New York: Natural History Press.

Cavalli-Sforza, L. L., and M. W. Feldman. 1981. *A Theory of Cultural Evolution: Cultural Transmission.* Princeton: Princeton Univ. Press.

Cloninger, C. R., and S. Yokoyama. 1981. The Channeling of Social Behavior. *Science* 213: 749–51.

Conrad, J. 1964. *The Many Worlds of Man.* New York: Crowell.

Crawshaw, L. I., et al. 1981. The Evolutionary Development of Vertebrate Thermoregulation. *Amer. Sci.* 69:543–50.

Davidson, E. H., and R. J. Britten. 1979. Regulation of Gene Expression: Possible Role of Repetitive Sequences. *Science* 209: 1052–59.

Dawkins, R. 1976. *The Selfish Gene.* New York: Oxford Univ. Press.

Dethier, V. G. 1982. The Selfish Nervous System. In *Changing Concepts of the Nervous System,* ed. A. Morrison and P. Struck. New York: Academic Press.

DeVoto, B., ed. 1974. *Mark Twain: Letters from the Earth.* New York: Harper & Row.

Dobzhansky, Th. 1970. *Genetics of the Evolutionary Process.* New York: Columbia Univ. Press.

Dyson, F. J. 1971. Energy in the Universe. *Sci. Amer.* 224:51–59.

Ehrensvärd, G. 1962. *Life: Origin and Development.* Chicago: Univ. of Chicago Press.

Fairbrother, N. 1956. *Men and Gardens.* New York: Knopf.

Bibliography

Frank, L. K. 1966. The World as a Communication Network. In *Sign, Symbol and Image,* ed. G. Kepes. New York: Braziller.

Frye, N. 1981. The Double Mirror. *Bull. Amer. Acad. Arts and Sciences* 35(3):32–41.

Fuller, R. B. 1938. *Nine Chains to the Moon.* Philadelphia: Lippincott.

Gamow, G. 1965. *Matter, Earth, and Sky.* 2d ed. Englewood Cliffs, N.J.: Prentice-Hall.

Garn, S. M. 1963. Culture and the Direction of Human Evolution. *Human Biology* 35:221–36.

Geertz, C. 1966. The Impact of the Concept of Culture on the Concept of Man. *Bull. Atomic Scientists* 22:2–8.

Gerard, R. 1960. Becoming: The Residue of Change. In *Evolution after Darwin: The Evolution of Man,* ed. S. Tax. Chicago: Univ. of Chicago Press.

———. 1961. Comments on Cultural Evolution. *Daedalus* 90 (3): 520.

Gould, S. J. 1977. *Ontogeny and Phylogeny.* Cambridge: Harvard Univ. Press.

———. 1980. This View of Life: Chance Riches. *Natural History* 89:36–44.

Hainsworth, F. R. 1981. Energy Regulation in Hummingbirds. *Amer. Sci.* 69:420–29.

Hockett, C. F. 1960. The Origin of Speech. *Sci. Amer.* 23:88–96.

Hoebel, E. A. 1960. The Nature of Culture. In *Man, Culture and Society,* ed. H. L. Shapiro. New York: Oxford Univ. Press.

Howells, W. W. 1973. *Evolution of the Genus Homo.* Reading, Mass.: Addison-Wesley Pub. Co.

Huxley, J. 1942. *Evolution: The Modern Synthesis.* London: Allen & Unwin.

Isaac, G. 1979. The Food-Sharing Behavior of Protohuman Hominids. In *Human Ancestors,* ed. G. Isaac and R. E. Leakey. San Francisco: Freeman.

Jacob, F. 1977. Evolution and Tinkering. *Science* 196:1161–66.

Jerison, H. J. 1976. Paleoneurology and the Evolution of Mind. *Sci. Amer.* 234:90–101.

Johanson, J., and M. Edey. 1981. *Lucy: The Beginnings of Mankind.* New York: Simon & Schuster.

King, M-C., and A. C. Wilson. 1975. Evolution at Two Levels in Humans and Chimpanzees. *Science* 188:107–16.

Langer, S. 1957. *Philosophy in a New Key: A Study in the Symbolism of Reason, Rite and Art.* 3d ed. Cambridge: Harvard Univ. Press.

Leakey, R. E., and R. Lewin. 1977. *Origins: What New Discoveries Reveal About the Emergence of Our Species and Its Possible Future.* New York: E. P. Dutton.

Lenski, G., and J. Lenski. 1978. *Human Societies: An Introduction to Macrosociology.* 3d ed. New York: McGraw-Hill.

Lewis, H. 1973. The Origin of Diploid Neospecies of Clarkia. *Amer. Nat.* 107:161–70.

Lovejoy, C. O. 1981. The Origin of Man. *Science* 211:341–50.

Luckett, W. P., ed. 1980. *Biology and Evolutionary Relationship of Tree Shrews.* New York: Plenum.

Lumsden, C. J., and E. O. Wilson. 1981. *Genes, Mind and Culture: The Coevolutionary Process.* Cambridge: Harvard Univ. Press.

McAlister, R. A. 1981. *Thomas McGlynn: Priest and Sculptor.* Providence, R.I.: Providence College Press.

Martin, R. D., 1981. Relative Brain Size and Basal Metabolic Rate. *Nature* (London) 293:57.

Marshall, J. T., and E. R. Marshall. 1976. Gibbons and Territorial Songs. *Science* 193:235–37.

Miller, J. G. 1965. Living Systems: Cross-Level Hypotheses. *Behavioral Science* 10 (4): 380–411.

Mills, D. R., et al. 1973. The Complete Nucleotide Sequence of a Replicating Molecule. *Science* 180:916–27.

Morowitz, H. J. 1968. *Energy Flow in Biology.* New York: Academic Press.

———. 1978. *Foundations of Bioenergetics.* New York: Academic Press.

Murdock, G. P. 1960. How Culture Changes. In *Man, Culture and Society,* ed. H. Shapiro. New York: Oxford Univ. Press.

Naef, A. 1926. Über die Urformen der Anthropomorphen und die Stammesgeschichte des Menschenschädes. *Naturwiss* 14:445–52.

Pederson, T. 1981. Messenger RNA Biosynthesis and Nuclear Structure. *Amer. Sci.* 69:76–84.

Potter, V. R. 1964. Society and Science. *Science* 146:1018–22.

———. 1971. *Bioethics: Bridge to the Future.* Englewood Cliffs, N.J.: Prentice-Hall.

Pribram, K. H. 1980. The Role of Analogy in Transcending Limits in the Brain Sciences. *Daedalus* 109:19–38.

Raup, D. M. 1979. Size of the Permo-Triassic Bottleneck and Its Evolutionary Implications. *Science* 206:217–18.

Romer, A. S. 1954. *Man and the Vertebrates.* Vol. 1. London: Pelican Books.

———. 1968. *The Procession of Life.* New York: World Publishing.

Sagan, C. 1977. *The Dragons of Eden: Speculations on the Evolution of Human Intelligence.* New York: Random House.

Savage-Rumbaugh, E. S., et al. 1978. Symbolic Communication between Two Chimpanzees *(Pan troglodytes). Science* 201:641–44.

———. 1980. Do Apes Use Language? *Amer. Sci.* 68:49–61.

Seyforth, R. M., et al. 1980. Monkey Responses to Three Different Alarm Calls: Evidence of Predator Classification and Semantic Communication. *Science* 210:801–3.

Shklar, J. N. 1980. Learning without Knowing. *Daedalus* 109 (2): 53–72.

Sibatani, A. 1980. The Japanese Brain. *Science* 207:22–27.

Simpson, G. G. 1967. *The Meaning of Evolution: A Study of the History of Life and of Its Significance for Man.* Rev. ed. New Haven: Yale Univ. Press.

Sinsheimer, R. L. 1971. The Brain of Pooh: An Essay on the Limits of Mind. *Amer. Sci.* 59:20–28.

Slobodkin, L. B. 1964. The Strategy of Evolution. *Amer. Sci.* 52: 342–57.

Smith, H. W. 1961. *From Fish to Philosopher.* Garden City, N.Y.: Doubleday.

Stadler, L. J. 1954. The Gene. *Science* 120:811–19.

Stanley, S. M. 1979. *Macroevolution: Pattern and Process.* San Francisco: Freeman.

———. 1981. *The New Evolutionary Timetable: Fossils, Genes, and the Origin of Species.* New York: Basic Books.

Stebbins, G. L. 1969. *The Basis of Progressive Evolution.* Chapel Hill: Univ. of North Carolina Press.

Stevenson, R. L. 1888. Pulvis et Umbra. *Scribner's Magazine.*

Steward, J. H. 1960. Evolutionary Principles and Social Types. In *Evolution after Darwin: The Evolution of Man*, ed. S. Tax. Chicago: Univ. of Chicago Press.

Swanson, C. P. 1973. *The Natural History of Man*. Englewood Cliffs, N.J.: Prentice-Hall.

——— et al. 1981. *Cytogenetics: The Chromosome in Division, Inheritance and Evolution*. Englewood Cliffs, N.J.: Prentice-Hall.

Swanson, C. P., and P. L. Webster. 1977. *The Cell*. 4th ed. Englewood Cliffs, N.J.: Prentice-Hall.

Swenson, May. 1978. *New & Selected Things Taking Place*. Boston: Little, Brown and Co.

Tanner, N. M. 1981. *On Becoming Human*. Cambridge: Cambridge Univ. Press.

Tucker, V. A. 1975. The Energetic Cost of Moving About. *Amer. Sci.* 63:413–19.

van den Bergh, A. 1981. Size and Age of the Universe. *Science* 213: 825–30.

von Foerster, H. 1966. From Stimulus to Symbol: The Economy of Biological Computation. In *Sign, Symbol and Image*, ed. G. Kepes. New York: Braziller.

White, E., and D. Brown. 1973. *The First Man*. New York: Time-Life Books.

White, L. A. 1959. *The Evolution of Culture*. New York: McGraw-Hill.

White, L., Jr. 1962. *Medieval Technology and Social Change*. New York: Oxford Univ. Press.

Wilson, E. O. 1975. *Sociobiology: The New Synthesis*. Cambridge: Harvard Univ. Press.

———. 1978. *On Human Nature*. Cambridge: Harvard Univ. Press.

———. 1981. Epigenesis and the Evolution of Social Systems. *Jour. Heredity* 72:70–77.

Wilson, P. J. 1980. *Man, the Promising Primate: The Conditions of Human Evolution*. New Haven: Yale Univ. Press.

Yunis, J. J., et al. 1980. The Striking Resemblance of High-Resolution G-Banded Chromosomes of Man and Chimpanzee. *Science* 208: 1146–48.

Ziman, J. 1968. *Public Knowledge: An Essay Concerning the Social Dimension of Science*. Cambridge: Cambridge Univ. Press.

Index

Index

brainwashing, 124
Brooks, V. W., 89, 152
Brown, D., 52, 54, 156
Butzer, K. W., 32, 152

Cambrian, 37
Campbell, B., 29, 58, 91, 92, 152
cannibalism, 139
Cannon, W., 13, 85, 96, 117, 152
Caplan, A. L., 152
care, parental, 51
Carr, A., 43, 152
caste system, 116
Cavalli-Sforza, L. L., 9, 113, 123, 124, 139, 152
celibacy, 139, 140
cell, ancestral, 28
Cenozoic, 35, 50
central nervous system, 8, 38, 44, 46, 57, 60, 63, 88, 107, 114, 124, 131, 140
cereals, 146
cerebrum, 50
change
  dampening of, 137
  patterns of, 147, 148, 151
  social, 156
channelling, 133
chaos, 12, 26, 66, 101, 135, 138
  and freedom, 31. See also disorder; diversity
chimpanzees, 51, 53, 55, 56, 102, 106, 144, 154
  brain size, 58
  genetic relation to humans, 33
  symbolic communication, 155
  vocal anatomy, 52
chlorophyll, 84
chordates, 39
Christianity, as a socioallele, 122
chromosomes, 7, 8, 33, 74, 111, 121, 123, 156
circulation, blood, 49
civilizations, 152
Clarkia, 79, 154
Cloninger, C. R., 119, 140, 152
code
  triplet, 70, 81
  universality of genetic, 22
coevolution, 119, 140, 146
cold-bloodedness, 49

collarbone, 55
complementarity of DNA, 67, 69, 76, 81
complexity, 19, 73, 75
concepts, 96, 151
  as cultural guidelines, 30
conceptualization, 47, 108, 111
control mechanisms, 90, 92, 106, 117. See also homeostasis
coordination, muscular, 50
copy-errors of DNA, 76, 78, 110, 112, 115, 116
cortex, cerebral, 46, 48
cosmology, 14
  and evolution, 18–20
cotton, 27
Crawshaw, L. I., 85, 152
Cretaceous, 27, 45
crop rotation, 145
crossing-over, 123
crystals, 110
cultigen, 91
culture, 3, 6, 31, 34, 35, 61, 108, 137, 151, 153, 156
  as an adaptive strategy, 30, 100
  coded information of, 34
  concepts, 28–31
  as control mechanisms, 84
  as an ecological system, 32
  Eskimo, 127
  as an evolutionary innovation, 100, 101, 107
culturgen, 90–91, 140
customs, 66, 125
cytogenetics, 156

Darwin, C., 9, 107
Dawkins, R., 11, 78, 86, 92, 111, 121, 139, 152
DeKooning, W., 139
dentition, 49
deoxyribose nucleic acid (DNA), 8–10, 79, 80, 84, 95, 105, 127, 148
  as a genetic language, 104
  method of deciphering, 71
  repair mechanisms, 76
  silent, 99
  structure and function, 67–70
Dethier V. G., 7, 139, 152

development
  authority-accepting stage of, 116
  cognitive, 116
  neotenous, 57, 61
  devices, enabling. See retrieval of information
Devonian, 41
DeVoto, B., 41, 152
dietary habits, 3
differentiation, 77, 95
diffusion, 126–28
  of ideas, 127. See also introgression
dinosaurs, 43–45
discrimination, visual, 48
disorder, 109, 113. See also chaos
displacement, 145
diversity, 113
  cultural, 31
  relation to evolution, 114
division
  cell, 77–79, 112
  of labor, 31, 62, 63
  nuclear, 77
Dobzhansky, Th., 27, 152
doctrine of special creation, 127
dogma, institutionalization of, 116
domestication of plants and animals, 146
dominance, sensory, 47
Dyson, F. J., 21, 152

ecotypes, 136
Edey, M., 11, 153
egg, relation to invasion of land, 42, 43
Ehrensvärd, G., 14, 152
Einstein, A., 122
elements, formation of heavy, 18
elephant, 143, 144
Eliot, T. S., 65
embryo, human, 55
embryogenesis, 33
emotion, 108
encephalization, 37, 38, 40, 63, 131
  relation to origin of culture, 38
energy, 20, 21, 72, 153, 154, 156

Index

Index

poets as symbolizers, 98
polyploidy, 14, 27
polytheism, 122
Pope, A., 36
posture, 44, 49, 106
Potter, V. R., 109, 137, 154, 155
pre-Pleistocene, 100
pressure
  cultural, 110
  selection, 118, 125, 130, 132
prey-predator relationship, 43
Pribram, K. H., 13, 155
primates, 15, 50, 53, 108, 120, 132
procreation, 140
prosimians, 47, 50
proteins, 71, 74, 81, 83
Protestantism, 122
protohumans, 98
purpose, 149

querezas, 102
quadripedalism, 53

radiation
  adaptive, 44, 50
  microwave, 20
randomness. *See* entropy
rats, 144
Raup, D. M., 27, 155
reality, 5, 48, 65, 96, 114
receptivity, continuous sexual, 61, 62
receptors, sensory, 94
recombination, 107, 112
red blood cell, 79
regulation, patterns of, 33
religions, 138
Rembrandt, 139
replication, 12, 21, 70, 77, 79, 80
  error, 72, 73, 111, 112, 125
  of sociogenes, 111, 112, 116
replicators, 78, 79, 111
reproduction, 10, 51, 66, 77, 78
reptiles, 41, 44, 45
retrieval of information (enabling devices), 90, 95, 108, 116, 134, 150
ribose nucleic acid (RNA), 8, 79
  of culture, 96
  heterogeneous (hnRNA), 81
  messenger (mRNA), 71, 80, 82
  ribosomal (rRNA), 71, 80, 82
  transfer (tRNA), 71, 80, 82
ribosomes, 80, 82, 83

rites of passage, 31
ritualization, 116
rituals, 128, 138
  as DNA of society, 92
Romer, A. S., 37–39, 41, 42, 45, 49, 155
rye, 126

Sagan, C., 11, 155
Saint Paul, 138
Savage-Rumbaugh, E. S., 99, 155
segregation of genes, 122–26
selection, 113, 139, 140
  artificial, 24, 126, 127
  cultural, 3, 140
  natural, 21, 22, 27, 71, 72, 76, 109, 127, 136, 140
self-awareness, 131, 132
self-maintenance, 79
self-perpetuation, 78
self-preservation, 78, 79
senses, 44, 47, 48, 50
Seyforth, R. M., 102, 155
Shakers, 140
sharks, 37
Shklar, J. N., 132, 155
shrews, 45, 143, 144
  tree, 50, 154
siamiangs, 102
Sibatani, A., 4, 155
signals, 93, 94, 97, 101–6, 109
  vs. symbols, 32, 33
Silk, J., 15, 17–19, 151
Simpson, G. G., 24, 155
Sinsheimer, R. L., 3, 155
skeleton, 39
Slobodkin, L. B., 16, 86, 101, 155
smell, 47
Smith, H. W., 24, 37, 155
society, membership in, 108
sociobiology, 152. 156
sociofacts, 91, 92
sociogenes, 34, 87, 93, 95–101, 108–11, 114–22, 135, 140, 141
sociogenotype, 34, 87, 94, 108, 111, 124, 125, 136, 137, 150
sociophenotype, 90, 94, 95, 97, 122
solar system, 131
songs, territorial, 102, 154
space, interstellar, 20
spear, 145
speech, 47, 52, 153

stability, organizational, 85
Stadler, L. J., 88, 118, 155
Stanley, S. M., 27, 62, 155
stars, 15
status quo, maintenance of, 117
Stebbins, G. L., 24, 73, 155
stegosaur, 44
Stern, I., 4, 5
Stevenson, R. L., 36, 155
Steward, J. H., 12, 156
stirrup, 145
stress, 137
sugar, right-handed, 131
supernovae, 18
supernaturalism, 66
Swanson, C. P., 58, 68, 70, 77, 82, 90, 111, 121, 156
Swenson, M., 156
symboling, 29, 96, 100, 101, 105
symbolism, 114
symbols, 4, 5, 7, 8, 32, 33, 96–101
  as enabling devices, 96, 105
  plasticity of, 109
symmetry, 38
syntax, 96, 103

tadpoles, 41
Tanner, N. M., 11, 32, 60–63, 106, 156
teaching, 107, 149
technology, 141, 156
therapsids, 45
thermodynamics, second law of, 20
thermoregulation, vertebrate, 152
think tanks, 139
time, 14, 17
tobacco, 27
tools, 3, 61, 63, 135, 144
traditions, 66, 125
transcription, 10, 71, 74, 79, 80–83, 87, 95, 115
translation, 10, 71, 74, 79, 82, 83, 87, 95, 115
transmission
  cultural, 124, 125, 152
  genetic, 112
  horizontal, 124
  oral, 116
  of sociogenes, 111, 112, 116, 117
  vertical, 124
Triassic, 27
Triticale, 126

Library of Congress Cataloging in Publication Data
Swanson, Carl P.
Ever-expanding horizons.
Bibliography: p.
Includes index.
1. Human evolution.   2. Social evolution.   I. Title.
GN281.4.S96   1983   573.2   82–21750
ISBN 0–87023–391–2
ISBN 0–87023–392–0 (pbk.)